REAWAKENING
the
HUMAN
SPIRIT

Other Books by Lance Secretan

The Bellwether Effect: Stop Following. Start Inspiring

A Love Story: An Intensely Personal Memoir

*The Spark, the Flame, and the Torch:
Inspire Self. Inspire Others. Inspire the World.*

ONE: The Art and Practice of Conscious Leadership

Inspire! What Great Leaders Do

Spirit@Work: Bringing Spirit and Values to Work

Inspirational Leadership: Destiny, Calling and Cause

*Reclaiming Higher Ground: Creating Organizations
That Inspire the Soul*

Living the Moment: A Sacred Journey

The Way of the Tiger: Gentle Wisdom for Turbulent Times

The Masterclass: Modern Fables for Working and Living

*Managerial Moxie: The 8 Proven Steps to Empowering
Employees and Supercharging Your Company*

CDs by Lance Secretan

ONE: The Art and Practice of Conscious Leadership: An Intensive 7-Day Audio Retreat

Inspire! What Great Leaders Do

Inspirational Leadership: Destiny, Calling and Cause

Reclaiming Higher Ground: Creating Organizations That Inspire the Soul

Living the Moment: A Sacred Journey

The Keys to the CASTLE: The Magic of Higher Ground Leadership

The New Story of Leadership: Reclaiming Higher Ground

Values-centered Leadership: A Model for Work and Life

The Calling Meditation

Videos and DVDs by Lance Secretan

The DreamQuest®: The Journey to Higher Ground DVD Series

Inspire! What Great Leaders Do

Inspirational Leadership: Destiny, Calling and Cause

Reclaiming Higher Ground: Creating Organizations That Inspire the Soul

The Keys to the CASTLE: The Magic of Higher Ground Leadership

Values-centered Leadership: A Model for Work and Life

LANCE SECRETAN

REAWAKENING *the* HUMAN SPIRIT

Finding the **SPARK**, the **FLAME**, and the **TORCH** Within

The Secretan Center Inc.

Library and Archive Canada

Secretan, Lance H. K.

Reawakening the Human Spirit: Finding the Spark, the Flame, and the Torch Within. / Lance Secretan.

ISBN 978-1-989207-01-7

1. Inspiration 2. Self-actualization (Psychology)
3. Personal development. I. Title.

Cover design: Kim Monteforte, WeMakeBooks.ca

Text design: Beth Crane, WeMakeBooks.ca

Printed in Canada

**The following terms, appearing in this book,
are registered trademarks of The Secretan Center Inc.:**

Higher Ground Leadership®
Inspirational Leadership®
Values-centered Leadership®
ONEDream®
Why-Be-Do®
The CASTLE® Principles
Spirit@Work®

"Know Thyself" was written over the portal of the antique world. Over the portal of the new world, "Be Thyself" shall be written.

— *Oscar Wilde*

Table of Contents

• • •

Acknowledgments

• • •

It is a Divine gift that the following souls have graced my journey and helped steward the ideas in these Reflections into a philosophy of life—and now a book.

Wisdom Circle members Claude Cloutier, Stewart Desson, Harvey Foote, Susan Grindle, Ryan Hellman, Victor Heredia, Julie Klein Petersen, Dianne McCallister, and Pamela Spiszman,

Fellow Pathfinders who live and teach Higher Ground Leadership® have joined me in creating a new movement to "Create a More Inspired World": Arnie Wohlgemut, Bill Richardson, Carlye Watson, Charlotte Seefeldt, Claudette Ward Holt, Colin Platt, David Fisher, David Sherrod, Deanna Stull, Eirini Metaxas, Ellen Brakel, Jan de Zwarte, Janet Palmer, Jeff Altman, Jerret Perry, Jim Rink, Karen Senteio, Kerri Balliet, Kevork Garabedian, Klaus-Peter Finke-Härkönen Lauren Flannagan, Len Rothman, Lynnette Embree, Lynnea Hagen, Nancy James, Rileagh Chase, Rod Stilwell, Ron Hulse, Sarah McErlean, Scott Regan, Steve Hultquist, Stewart Desson, Sue Lindsay, Tim May, Tony Martignetti, Victor Heredia, Whitney Higdon.

Thanks to Alise Cortez, Stephan Hein, Hart Hillman, Marie Knapp, Eric Simmons, Lue Siray, Roger Steinkruger, Bill Todd and the many friends, students and clients (same thing) who have helped shape my thinking over the years.

Simone Gabbay has been kneading my prose for many years, in many languages, and with many books, and has done so once again—she is a true professional and much more than an editor.

Heidy Lawrance, and the team at Heidy Lawrance Associates, have been shepherds of the design process, and Fred Cheetham of Friesens, has offered incomparable printing and production services. Kudos to Allan Thornton, who translates the ideas presented in this book into a website and Jack Werner who does the same with multi-media shows.

I am in love with two people – one who is no longer on this do-main (my late wife, Tricia) and one who is (Barb Siray). Both have been fundamental forces in shaping who I am today, what I believe, how I live, and what I teach. Without them this book would not exist—I am so grateful for how they have augmented my love with their love and wisdom.

Introduction

• • •

I have dedicated my professional career to helping corporations, and their leaders, to build inspiring organizations, and I have been fortunate to learn from so many people on this journey. My attempt to capture what I had learned became the central theme of my earlier book, *The Spark, the Flame, and the Torch,* which I wrote for leaders, to help them reimagine the entire notion of leadership—replacing "industrial age" concepts with a commitment to becoming more inspired and inspiring for others. *This is what, I discovered,* **great** *leaders do.*

But my path has changed direction over the years because I discovered that when I shared this work with leaders, the organizations improved and became more successful and work cultures more inspiring, yet the fortunes of their employees did not improve in equal measure. Organizational success often meant personal "success" for leaders. In one notorious example, following years of disastrous mistakes, GE laid off 20,000 employees—not because employees had failed, but because management had. GE's CEO stood to earn $230 million in compensation in the same year that 20,000 souls lost their jobs. In a rare rebuke, GE's board of directors voted (in a non-binding resolution) to reject management's compensation recommendations.[1]

---

1 https://www.marketscreener.com/quote/stock/GENERAL-ELECTRIC-COMPANY-4823/news/GE-shareholders-reject-CEO-Culp-s-230-million-pay-in-rare-rebuke-33154952/?countview=0

I have come to realize that times have changed and the dramatic rise of spiritual poverty such experiences have caused is being felt and expressed by so many, and this demands new answers.

Helping organizations to become more inspiring is not enough. Corporate incompetence and malfeasance, recessions, wars, terrorism, mass shootings, pandemics, declining mental health, drug and violence epidemics, and political crises have roiled society and accelerated the epidemic of our spiritual hunger. It is not just a corporate issue; it is a human issue.

What I have come to realize is that we have created an artificial reality—two separate worlds: business and the rest of our lives. I can go up to just about anybody I meet on the street and give them a hug, but I can't do that at work. I can tell *anyone* I love them—except at work. We exhort employees to accelerate their commitment to serving customers, while we overlook the need to do the same for employees, unions, regulators, vendors, and the general public—all the other humans on whom we depend to make everything work. We treat humans as "resources" and people who buy our products and services as "consumers," as if all these souls were merely production mechanisms. If we behaved this way with our friends, they would rightly scold us. We use jargon (granular, reach out, KPIs, taking this off-line) and approaches at work (Performance Appraisals, Engagement Surveys and "holding people accountable") that we would not dare use at home—would you hold your spouse accountable? Or give your spouse a Performance Appraisal? We behave and have practices at work that would be foreign and hurtful in the rest of our lives. We are ruthless and competitive at work in ways that would be completely unacceptable at home. We have lost our humanity in Corporate America, and therefore, our inspiration. Too often we see examples of what I call "Exploitive Capitalism," which has caused disillusionment among people who see greed, shareholder demands, deceptive marketing practices, environmental ruthlessness, rapacious growth, and employee burnout[2] as the uninspiring norm.

During my presentations to audiences, I often ask them this question: "What percentage of the population do you think would leave the corporate world and pursue different interests if they had a completely free hand?" Like at an auction, I start at 50 percent and the audience will typically raise the offer until we settle at an estimate of something more than 80 percent. Why is this a tragedy? Because, apart from the human anguish and suffering that such a chronic state of discontent causes, we live in a capitalist society, one of whose main engines (besides the church and government) is commerce, and if we botch this critical source of livelihood and exchange, we risk losing everything. So, reclaiming our passion for corporate life, and reinfusing work with inspiration, is not an inconsequential issue.

Yet even this is not enough. We are people, just in different settings—home, work, play, and more, and the message is clear: the world is hurting, it is uninspiring for many people and some corporate organizations have become some of the least inspiring places on Earth and since so many of us work, this is a vital aspect of our lives. But we need to regain our inspiration everywhere, not just at work, and learn how to become inspired in a world that does not always feel inspiring across our entire lives. Just about every corner of society is hurting, and people at all levels and ages are yearning for the inspiration that seems to have evaporated from their lives.

---

2 You can test your own level of burnout with this free quiz:
  https://secretan.com/assessment-tools/burnout-survey/

The answers to these issues are not just "corporate solutions," they are human and spiritual solutions.

I have been especially struck by the intense and growing need of everyone I meet, for something they can believe in, something that demands and engages their deepest longings. People seek to ensure that their lives are fueled by passion, have meaning, and that they are needed in the world. As Frederick Buechner reminds us, "The place God calls you to is the place where your deep gladness and the world's deep hunger meet." This passion-fueled desire and the awareness of the opportunities available to serve are the source of people's inspiration, from which they create the energy that inspires those with whom they connect and relate. Opportunity may only knock once, but passion leans on the doorbell.

So many people quite rightly told me that *The Spark, the Flame and the* Torch had a message that *everyone* needed to hear and live, but that it was too narrowly focused on "corporate" life. And so, although the book you now hold in your hands draws heavily on this original work, it has been completely rewritten to address the *entirety of our lives*. I hope you will consider this as a personal life manual for you, and a roadmap to inspiration for people of all ages, everywhere. I hope that it can become a manual for you as you help the world reclaim its humanness, its capacity to be inspiring and inspired by life. It is in your hands and the hands of all of us.

We Are All Leaders

The overarching name for the work described in this book is "Higher Ground Leadership®"[3]. I use the term *leadership* in its broadest sense—we are all leaders—at home, at work, as citizens,

---

3 https://secretan.com/about-us/higher-ground-leadership/

and at school. Higher Ground Leadership® is a breakthrough philosophy that enables others to achieve a unique sense shared by too few people—*inspiration*. It is built on the simple concept (seldom practiced, because it is not always easy) that inspired people create inspired families and inspired organizations, which create inspired communities, which create inspired countries, which inspire the world.

We have been using fear-based theories of motivation for centuries. But this overlooks the deep human need to be inspired more than motivated—and there is a big difference between the two.[4] People are yearning to be inspired and to be a part of families and communities that are inspiring, to elect and follow politicians who are inspiring, to work for inspiring people and teams who build inspiring places to live, work, and play, based on values, meaning and fulfillment. We are yearning for inspiration in our marriages, families, churches, communities, with our friends, and in the media and our entertainment. The reality is, we are looking for inspiration everywhere, and anywhere we can find it. To create inspiring relationships and environments though, we must first become inspired ourselves, for we cannot give what we do not have within us. We cannot inspire others unless we are first inspired ourselves. **This is the Spark.**

Once we have become inspired ourselves, we are then able to inspire others using our own deep wells of inspiration. This is how great things are achieved—not just by understanding this, but, more importantly, by living as inspiring people and practicing the principles and values that are vital to each of us and cause others to be inspired too. We reach for greatness when we are inspired to do so. Our role in life is to be the light for others—to be *their* inspiration. **This is the Flame.**

---

4 See this video about the difference between motivation and inspiration:
   https://www.youtube.com/watch?v=kr725Lm7bfM

Just as important is the role of each of us, our families and communities, our organizations, and our society, to create a legacy—to mentor, lead, coach and teach, to help people to grow, and to ensure that what we build makes a positive difference and lasts. This is how we change the world. *None of us will live forever, but our aspiration should be to create something that will.* **This is the Torch.**

We are moving through unprecedented times of disillusionment and anxiety. According to the World Economic Forum, one in four people globally, will suffer from mental ill health in their lives and some 400 million are suffering today.[5] The National Institutes of Health reported that "Overall, more than 50% of the general population in middle- and high-income countries will suffer from at least one mental disorder at some point in their lives.[6] The "Great Resignation" during the Covid-19 pandemic recalibrated how people felt about work, with millions quitting toxic workplaces. A report from NBC revealed that "The number of children ages 6–12 who visited children's hospitals for suicidal thoughts or self-harm has more than doubled since 2016, according to data from 46 such facilities across the country collected for NBC News by the Children's Hospital Association, a trade organization."[7] A book could be filled with similar statistics.

People are hurting—financially, spiritually, emotionally, and physically. Our culture has evolved into one that brilliantly rewards the metrics of performance while overlooking the measures of the heart, and this has caused an evaporation of inspiration. Consequently, we have been living through what has been referred to as "the Decade from Hell," and there is a yearning for a new beginning, an opportunity to create and enjoy a brighter future—a second "Age of Enlightenment."

5 https://www.weforum.org/agenda/2018/11/five-ways-mental-health-care-better-depression/
6 https://www.ncbi.nlm.nih.gov/pmc/articles/PMC5007565/
7 https://www.nbcnews.com/news/us-news/suicidal-thoughts-are-increasing-young-kids-experts-say-it-began-n1263347

There is a growing movement that seeks to restore joy, significance, and personal worth in life. It is a movement formed by those who are leaving old and barren ideas of self-focus and power, attempting to salve the soul with endless consumption and materialism. This awakening is embracing new philosophies that inspire others to get things done, to have fun and to live meaningful and fulfilling lives. As Sir Richard Branson reminds us, "As soon as something stops being fun, I think it's time to move on. Life is too short to be unhappy. Waking up stressed and miserable is not a good way to live."

Why do some people seem to have an aura about them, a presence, an ability to inspire others that gets things done and enables them to live meaningful and fulfilled lives? What makes them special, extraordinary, happy, and delightful to be around? Since we have all the information, tools, and skills necessary to live an inspired life, why don't we all live in this way?

When the Dalai Lama was asked what surprised him most about humanity, he answered, "Man! Because he sacrifices his health in order to make money. Then he sacrifices money to recuperate his health. And then he is so anxious about the future that he does not enjoy the present; the result being that he does not live in the present or the future; he lives as if he is never going to die, and then dies having never really lived."

There is an antidote to all this unhappiness—it is *inspiration*. This quote is often attributed to Lao Tzu: "If you are depressed, you are living in the past. If you are anxious you are living in the future. If you are at peace you are living in the present." When we are inspired, we are living in the present. We cannot be inspired and depressed at the same time. Different biochemicals present themselves within our bodies when we are inspired (a topic we will explore later), causing the biochemicals associated with sadness or depression to lose their capacity to dominate our bodies or energy. Often, one of the ways we can become inspired is to serve. Suppose your girlfriend stands you up on your first date. You have a choice about how you will react. You can go home, feel sorry for yourself, and get drunk, indulge in binge-eating or TV watching, or drugs. Or you can visit a friend and help them paint their bedroom. Painting the walls may not be your favorite thing to do, but deepening your friendship, receiving gratitude and love for your contribution, and the satisfaction of a job well done, will pull you out of yourself. Yes, you had a bad day, but you helped someone else have a good one—and this caused you to be inspired, too. The days when we are most inspired are the days when we serve, when we feel alive, experience meaning, fulfillment and joy, and this feeling causes us to brighten the lives of others.

The Spark Ignites the Flame, and the Flame Lights the Torch

In Part One—The Foundation, we will explore how we can become more open to change. We will review the phases of learning, growth and change, and how to establish an open mindset which is essential to transformation. We will review how we misunderstand the concept of stress. We will also explore the difference between motivation and inspiration, explaining the two aspects of ourselves—our *Social Self* and our *Essential Self.* We will also review the concepts of inclusion and oneness. These foundational concepts will prepare us for the learnings in the twelve "Reflections" that follow in Parts Two, Three, and Four.

In Part Two—The Spark: Inspiring Self, we will explore the concept of the *Spark*—the initial energy that kindles the embers of inspiration within each of us, that moves us to live large and to inspire others, to reach our highest potential, to make a meaningful difference in our own life, the lives of others, and the world. We must first *become* inspired (the Spark) in order to inspire others. Without the spark, we are ordinary and dull, and we aim below our promise. This dullness is the absence of passion and energy, of dreams and magic in our lives, of relationships that inspire, and of bearings and paths that lead to meaning and fulfillment, excitement, and zest. The spark initiates fusion, combustion, and reaction. The spark is awakened by a newly realized, deep inner awareness of **Why** we are here on Earth, how we will **Be** while we are here, and what we have been called upon to **Do**. Few people have discovered the answers to these questions or have even cared to explore them. They are content to live the unexamined life, and as Socrates said, "The unexamined life is not worth living." On the other hand, those who have reflected thoughtfully on these questions and defined the right answers for themselves, have ignited the spark within them. In this way we listen to our often-silenced inner voice to create what we call the *Why-Be-Do*®—**Why** we are here, how we will **Be**, and what we will **Do**. When you stand in the presence of someone who has a deep, inner knowing of who they are—an awareness of **Why** they are here on Earth, how they will **Be** while they are here, and what they have been called to **Do**—you are standing in the presence of an inspiring person. This is the "spark" that flashes and radiates from within them. Their certainty about their path, and the passion they have for it, makes them the kind of person that others want to be with and to follow, firing up their own hopes for living the same way. This inner awareness creates a fusion with their higher purpose and causes a powerful release of energy. It causes them to be inspiring—they can't help themselves, because it radiates from within them and stirs the hearts of others.

We fill up our own "inspiration well" by building and nurturing inspiring relationships (like painting a friend's bedroom—*service.*) You will be guided through interactive exercises that enable you to build inspiring relationships. And you will learn how to craft your ONE-Dream® that ignites your passion—your Why-Be-Do®—a dream that can transform your life from black-and-white to Technicolor®.

In Part Three—The Flame: Inspiring Others, we will discover how *the spark ignites the flame.* We will explore the "Flame"—the fire within us that lights the way for others, that generates intensity and raises the temperature, that fires the spiritual and emotional rockets of our lives, that takes us to unexplored places of promise. The flame is bright and visible to all—it represents the values we practice, and passionately believe in, and that we model for others. The flame fuels a fervor that informs all our actions and illuminates the path for others. It is our standard against which we calibrate our conduct. It represents the behaviors we model for others and teach to them, and which, in turn, encourages them to ignite their own spark and add their own fire to their flame. The flame is ignited when we live a set of values we call the CASTLE® Principles—"CASTLE®" is an acronym for six inspiring ways of being:

- *Courage*: Reaching beyond the boundaries of our existing limitations, fears, and beliefs
- *Authenticity*: Being genuine, transparent, and aligned with our inner voice in all aspects of life
- *Service*: Willing, and actively supporting, the good of the other
- *Truthfulness*: Being honest and transparent in all thoughts, words, and actions

- *Love*: Relating to others by touching their hearts in ways that add to who we both are as persons
- *Effectiveness*: Achieving desired outcomes successfully

As we live by these principles, we are the flame by which others are warmed, guided, developed, comforted, and inspired, because people love others who are courageous, authentic, serving, truthful, loving and effective. This is how we inspire others.

In Part Four—The Torch: Inspiring the World, we will explore how t*he flame lights the torch.* The "Torch" is the legacy we create and the wisdom we pass on, the gift of mentoring, coaching, and contributing to the growth, hope and happiness of others—how we convert the spark into a flame, using it to light the torch, which we share with others. The flame is used to light the torch, and the torch is used to carry fire to others. The torch is "paying it forward," teaching others, serving them, and helping them to grow, and being an inspiring mentor for them. It is with our torch that we light the way for others. This is how we change the world. As Carl Jung reminded us, "As far as we can discern, the sole purpose of human existence is to kindle a light in the darkness of mere being."

To live the inspired and inspiring life, we pass through these three progressions: We become inspired: *the Spark*; We live an inspiring life that inspires others: *the Flame*; and we share with others the opportunity to do the same: *the Torch.*

We can all get there, but first we have to do the work. Let's begin.

....

You never change things by fighting the existing reality.
To change something, create a new model that
makes the existing models obsolete.

Buckminster Fuller

....

PART ONE

The Foundation

Part One
The Foundation

● ● ●

In this section, we will review some ideas that will serve as useful concepts—a foundation—on which we will later build the philosophy that leads to an inspiring life—and world. We will introduce terms and concepts that will be referred to frequently as we travel together in the twelve Reflections that follow. One of the core ideas I propose is that *who* we are is what inspires us and others, not *what* we know, or how powerful, successful or influential we are. The purpose of this section, therefore, is to help set the ground on which the rest of this work is based, locating it firmly in *who* you are as an inspiring human being that others love, and are inspired by.

Learning

As you experience the ideas in this book, you will be encouraged to learn. Learning almost always requires us to replace existing knowledge with new information or wisdom, and therefore, learning is nearly always a challenge to the ego. Letting go of what we think we already know is the hardest of admissions. Learning has different phases that most of us pass through in sequence. This process is known as the *PIES Theory of Learning*.

Political (Motivation/Social Self)

Intellectual (Motivation/Social Self)

Emotional (Inspiration/Essential Self)

Spiritual (Inspiration/Essential Self)

4

We all tend to learn in four sequential levels and each level of learning deepens the understanding and the practice of what has previously been learned.

The first level is Political. Someone explains or teaches something to us, or we read some information and we register it in our mind. Initially, we may not be ready to fully embrace this new information. For example, someone might tell you that you should not throw your disposable plastic water bottle out of the car window because it creates garbage and messes up the environment. You might say to yourself, "This is silly. I'm just one person and my single water bottle won't make any difference." But you do not want to become known as a polluter, or to upset or lose the approval of your friends, so you reluctantly agree to refrain in future from discarding water bottles out of your car window. You don't fully buy into the idea, but you want to "fit in." You have just made a *political* decision, so your learning, at this stage, is superficial—merely political. Another example: a study by the London School of Hygiene and Tropical

Medicine at a gas-station toilet on a British highway revealed that users washed their hands more often when others were present in the washroom—a political decision based on participants' need to avoid the disapproval of others.

The second, deeper, level of learning is Intellectual. You discover that each day 60 million water bottles are thrown away, that it takes 700 years for these plastic bottles to degrade in a landfill, that about 100 million animals die each year from plastic waste, and that by 2050, there will be more plastic water bottles in the ocean than there are fish. You realize that if we continue to use and throw away all those water bottles, a major crisis will occur. So, you appreciate the logic of this new learning, understand the consequences, and you commit to adjusting your behavior. You have just made an *intellectual* decision and your learning is now a part of your intellectual, rational awareness.

The third, even deeper level of learning is Emotional. You start to notice discarded water bottles everywhere. You had not noticed this before. It seems many people are careless about this. You research this a bit more and discover that one million plastic water bottles are sold in the world every minute and only 10 percent of them are recycled. As you reflect on this, it occurs to you that this could become a global catastrophe, and since you are a nature lover, seeing discarded water bottles on your favorite walks in the park is concerning to you. Your deep connection to nature fuels your desire to become a proponent of keeping your used water bottles in the car and taking them home to place in your recycling bin. You have made an *emotional* commitment to *living* the new learning.

Finally, the fourth and deepest level of learning is Spiritual. At this point, your passion is so aroused you become a teacher of, and a missionary for, this new learning. You are passionate about the environment, and you don't want it to be harmed because you are part of nature too, and anything that hurts nature hurts you, because you believe you are one with the natural world. You are now infusing this learning at the deepest level—it is part of your spiritual core, which you embrace as part of who you are—and you become an evangelist. You have become a spiritual learner.

The PIES Learning journey moves us from learning from the outside to learning from the inside and from outer knowing to inner knowing.

As Galileo said, "You cannot teach a man anything. You can only help him discover it within himself." As you absorb the ideas in this book, ask yourself, "At what level am I learning this concept?" Try to bring it into your consciousness at the deepest level, paying attention to the ideas that you now hold, and which you may wish to re-examine so that you can make room for a new way of being. The old concepts have been your friends for a long time. Say goodbye to them, where appropriate, with gentleness and gratitude for how they have guided you up to now, and for how they gave you the platform on which to build new thinking.

Being open to new thinking requires a certain mindset. Carol Dweck, Lewis and Virginia Eaton Professor of Psychology at Stanford University, refers to this as a "growth mindset." She posits that there are two theories of intelligence, which she calls mindsets, that we each believe about our intellectual abilities (although we all can switch between the one or the other). People who possess a more fixed mindset believe that their intellectual abilities are set. They tend to approach learning by trying to appear smart, and they often try to avoid challenges because they are afraid that working hard at something or making mistakes sends a signal to others that they don't have high ability. On the other hand, those with more of a growth mindset believe that abilities can be developed—they are more likely to see effort and hard work as a method to accelerate learning and to see setbacks and failures as opportunities to build new skills.

Do you approach learning with a "growth mindset"? Are you open to letting go of what you are sure you know, and learning at the deepest, spiritual level? Even though, as I have mentioned earlier, learning is a challenge to the ego—the rewards for the curious are lifelong. As Albert Einstein pointed out, "It is not that I'm so smart. But I stay with the questions much longer." Asking questions is an essential part of learning. Isaac Newton was not the first person to notice an apple falling to the ground, but he was the first person to ask why it did so.

Inclusion and Oneness

7

Many people live with the illusion that we are separate. But it is an illusion—everything is connected.

Whenever we experience pain, hurt, loneliness, or sadness, it is because we have become separated from what, or whom, we love. And whenever we are inspired, happy, elated or joyful, it is because we are one with what, or whom, we love. All human challenges and successes can be explained through this awareness. We are as connected to each other and everything in the world as a wave is connected to the ocean.

Oneness attracts; separateness rejects. When we are in love with some-one, it is as if we are one: two souls, one flame. That is because we are.

When we love doing something, or something makes our hearts soar and we are inspired, we feel as if we are one with it, because we are.

When we ache over the imperiled state of nature or the rising level of violence in the world, we ache because we feel the same pain. We share it because we are one.

Oneness means including others because we are one with them—a discovery we make through the fourth level of learning in the PIES Theory of Learning we just reviewed. Being clear about who we are, living to a set of affirming values, and helping others to grow requires us to be inclusive—to honor the sacredness of others—regardless of their beliefs or faith. To exclude others causes us to be *un*inspired.

In addition to the distinction between religion and spirituality that is woven throughout this book, the notion of *inclusion* is equally important. As Garrison Keillor said, "Going to church no more makes you a Christian than sleeping in your garage makes you a car." And Gandhi said with less wit but more elegance, "There are no religions in Heaven." I seek not to offend anyone, but rather to include everyone, to embrace oneness, as the God I believe in has counseled me to do. Where I have referred to "God" or where "God" is referenced by others, please think of this as the God of your choice—Creator, the Divine, the Universe, or whatever has meaning for you.

Everything is connected—as Albert Einstein said, "A person experiences life as something separated from the rest—a kind of optical delusion of consciousness. Our task must be to free ourselves from this self-imposed prison, and through compassion, to find the reality of Oneness."

We cannot be inspiring or inspire others if we exclude them or disconnect from the whole. Exclusion creates pain and hurt and thus, is uninspiring. We are most inspiring when we incorporate a connection to a higher presence within ourselves, our work, and our aspirations—honoring the sacredness of everyone.

The world has become increasingly polarized, and differences of opinion—about race, religion, politics, democracy vs. authoritarianism, sexual orientation, and so much more—are a growing threat to our society and suck the oxygen from inspiration. Some seek to amplify their arguments and beliefs by insulting, name calling, and belittling those who hold differing views. But this is not inspiring. We may differ in our perspectives, but we are still one. You will still be my friend, and I will still be committed to inspiring you, even if we disagree. I can embrace you, while not embracing your opinion. A reasoned, respectful, and loving conversation can be held anywhere, at any time, on any subject, and I will still love you. But when you insult me, I shut down. This is fundamental science: Newton's Third Law states that for every action there is an equal and opposite reaction. If we spew vitriol, it will come back to us; if we show love, it will be returned. This is not rocket science—it is karma. We can raise the level of inspiration in our lives by practicing the art of discourse in ways that make the other person feel larger, not smaller. Every opinion can be held and respected, while we continue to respect the sacredness of those with differing views. Progress—and joy in our lives—occurs when you and I are one, not when we are separate.

We inspire others when we reduce the circle of those we exclude and widen the circle of those we include—until there is only one circle. As Howard Winters remarked, "Civilization is the process in which one gradually increases the number of people included in the term 'we' or 'us' and at the same time decreases those labeled 'you' or 'them' until that category has no one left in it." Inspiring others requires that we include them, not exclude them. As Edwin Markham wrote,

9

He drew a circle that shut me out;
Heretic, rebel, a thing to flout.
But love and I had the wit to win:
We drew a circle that took him in.

Stress

Stress is a subject that can be viewed through many lenses. In our society today, stress is often blamed for our unhappiness or depression. There are countless books and courses on "stress management," but the best cure for stress is not learning how to "manage" it, but to learn how to reframe events so that they are no longer causing stress. A Buddhist parable tells the story of a monk confronted by a fierce tiger while on a quiet walk. The monk becomes very still. He knows that just beyond him is a cliff and just below that cliff are the rocky shoreline and the turbulent sea. The monk is caught between the tiger and the sea, and so he chooses to lower himself over the cliff. Holding onto a thick vine, he is filled with gratitude that the vine sustains his weight. During his prayer, the monk notices a bright red, juicy strawberry growing on the cliff face. Looking up, the tiger is snarling at him. Looking down, the waves are crashing and pounding onto the rocks below. The monk breathes a breath of deep gratitude and plucks the strawberry from its vine and, putting it into his mouth, savors the moment.

Stress is like that. It exists if you let it. But it doesn't, if you don't.

If someone cuts you off as you enter the freeway, you have choices: you can rail, yell, curse and call the offender names, making sure he clearly understands what an idiot you think he is, while your heart races, your blood pressure rises, and you try to control your anger.

That is stress. Or you can take a breath, be grateful for your life, and let the other driver carry on with where they are going. It's your choice—you can choose stress, or you can choose detachment. And when we choose to be stressed, we transmit that negative energy to everyone with whom we connect—and this generally doesn't turn out well! Additionally, choosing stress lowers creativity, innovation and performance, and it is detrimental to our health, well-being and longevity. Stress, then, is counterproductive to all our best intentions in life. Stress is inspiration's assassin.

But it doesn't have to be, because we can choose to let situations that are potentially irritating or maddening to flow by us—Teflon instead of Velcro—it's our choice. Stress is a description of our reaction to an event. As Victor Frankel reminded us, "Between stimulus and response there is a space. In that space is our power to choose our response. In our response lies our growth and our freedom." He added, "Forces beyond your control can take away everything you possess except one thing, your freedom to choose how you will respond to the situation."[8] We can choose to be a victim, feel ground down, overworked, harassed and angry, and conclude that people and the world suck, or we can unlink our emotions from the event, smile, and enjoy what we are doing in the moment, and work to bring greater joy and inspiration to our immediate world, including the conditions that otherwise would cause us to be stressed. Stress, then, is something we *choose*, and we always have the option to make healthier—and more inspiring—choices. We each possess a limited amount of energy, which we can choose to channel positively or negatively. Stress is always negative; it is never inspiring. Where we

11

---

8 Victor E. Frankel, *Man's Search for Meaning*, Beacon Press; 1st edition (June 1, 2006) the book is a memoir of Frankl's imprisonment in concentration camps during World War II and a brief description of the principles of logotherapy, a school of psychotherapy that he founded.

direct our limited amount of life energy is a choice available to each of us. The light at the end of the tunnel is not an illusion, the tunnel is.

Here are some additional tips to help you remove stress from your life—and abandon it forever:

- Download the free Spirit@Work® Cards app available from the Apple and Google Play stores (QR Codes below; a paid upgrade is also available); pull a card each day and use it as your basis for meditation, reflection and personal renewal.

- Watch Lance Secretan's video on meditation and mindfulness: www.secretan.com/meditation
- Do you have a difficult boss or relationship? Check the BBC Dark Triad Personality Test: http://www.bbc.com/future/story/20151123-how-dark-is-your-personality
- Take the free Burnout Survey: https://secretan.com/higher-ground-leadership-members/burnout-survey/

How will you choose to react today? Do you choose stress? Or do you choose to let events that cause you to experience stress pass, breathe gently, and be grateful for being alive and enjoy the miracle that we call life? Such a world is available to us all. We cannot be inspired *and* stressed. Choosing to remove our angry or resentful reactions (stress) removes the barrier that would otherwise prevent us from following the path towards inspiration.

The Social Self and the Essential Self

We each make decisions based on one of two criteria: the ego or the soul—what I describe as the *social self* and the *essential self.* We will refer often to these in the pages ahead. The social self externally references, using "success" as a measure. The metric of success seeks to answer such questions as: Am I right? Will I win? Am I good enough? Will I get more (money, power, status, approval, fame)—all being externally gauged metrics. "More" is the signature of the social self, constantly searching for more "stuff" and approval. The social self—the persona, by which we are generally known to others—calibrates almost exclusively against the exterior—the material and the secular.

The essential self, on the other hand, references internally, using a different measure: "joy." The essential self is a deeper, numinous source that connects us to our higher selves. The metric of joy seeks to answer different questions such as: Will this serve others? Will this make the world a better place? How can I serve? Will this bring happiness? Is it beautiful, elegant and simple? Does this nourish my soul? All these are internally gauged metrics.[9] The essential self represents our true essence, our internal compass, what we long for and what, if supported generously by the social self, would guide us joyfully and flawlessly through our lives—as leaders and as people. But the social self constantly manipulates and overrides our thinking in order to make us conform to an external compass—what people will think and whether they will love or approve of us and our

13

---

9 Take the Secretan Center Inc. free Soulscreen Survey to determine whether your work is nourishing your soul: https://secretan.com/higher-ground-leadership-members/soulscreen

image, criticize us for our shortcomings, how we will be assessed or judged, what is politically correct, whether we will succeed or fail or be triumphant, or whether our actions will enhance our careers—in other words, our level of "success"—as judged by external measures. Eckhart Tolle writes, "Why does the ego play roles? Because of the one unexamined assumption, one fundamental error, one unconscious thought. That thought is: I am not enough. Other unconscious thoughts follow: I need to play a role in order to get what I need to be fully myself; I need to get more so that I can be more."[10] So, although our lives often succumb to the direction of the external compass of our social self—the outside measure—we yearn to be guided more authentically from the compass within, by our essential self—the inside measure. Inspiration cannot come from the social self; it is only to be found in the essential self.

14

The social self seeks to divide, compete and separate. The essential self seeks to love, unify and heal. The social self is concerned with "How do I look?" The essential self is concerned with "How do I feel?"

The essential self falls in love (the social self will try to tap into fear by dismissing this as infatuation, warning that the object of our desires is flawed, dangerous, unreliable, and sometimes unattractive). The essential self wants to make the world a better place, but the social self is more focused on social self-gratification. The social self seeks to motivate with fear, and those who seek to motivate others deliberately tap into the fears of the social self. The embers of inspiration are sourced from love and perpetually burn within the essential self, and those who seek to inspire others fan those embers into flames. The essential self unapologetically embraces idealism,

10 Eckhart Tolle, *A New Earth: Awakening to Your Life's Purpose*, Penguin; Reprint edition, January 30, 2008, Chapter 4, Role-playing: The Many Faces of the Ego, page 109.

seldom flinching when subjected to the criticism received from the social selves of others. Our best selves live in the essential self—and our ego lives in the social self.

The most frequent behavior of many people is one that emanates principally from the social self, typically characterized by ambition, determination, competition, aggression, and goal attainment, and this results in the dismal data of sadness, depression, despair and loneliness, ever present in our world and to which we referred earlier. Living a life that is inspiring, and that inspires others, requires that we listen to the essential self at least as often as we listen to the social self—hearing and respecting both. In other words, inspiring others and being inspired by them flows from joy more than success, from the essential self more than the social self. The unhealthy singular focus on the social self is why so many people give up their day jobs in exchange for the freedom, fulfillment, independence, and the pursuit of their dreams that beckon to them from the independent or entrepreneurial life. They are escaping leaders and companies that rely on the social self and are answering the call of their essential selves. The dominance of the social self is also why marriages fail, friendships atrophy, and most crimes occur.

The social self aggressively pursues self-gratifying ambition and goal attainment, and this results in the shallowness of life experienced by uninspired people. Living a life that is inspiring, and that inspires others, requires that we listen to the essential self at least as often, even more, than we listen to our personality—hearing and respecting both equally. In other words, inspiring others, and being inspired, flows from love and joy—not from fear and success—from the soul more than the ego. What your social self acquires can be stolen; but no one can take away what lives in your essential self.

The big question is this: "Who is speaking? Is it the social self, or the essential self?" When you make a decision, choose to hang out with a friend, accept a new job, make a purchase—ask these questions, and listen to which voice is whispering in your ear—the social self or the essential self. Lord Byron wrote, "There are four questions of value in life, Don Octavio. What is sacred? Of what is the spirit made? What is worth living for and what is worth dying for? The answer to each is the same. Only love." When you listen to the essential self—it is love speaking. Before reading on, watch this 3.5-minute video entitled, "Leading from the Soul": https://secret-an.com/leadingfromthesoul/.

Motivation

We have created confusion around the two words "motivation" and "inspiration." We think of them as interchangeable, as if they had the same meaning, but in reality, they are almost the exact opposite of each other, as I will show.

Very few people really understand the difference between motivation and inspiration. Motivation is something we *do* to people. It consists of a combination of two pressure points: fear (e.g., punishments, revenge, and reprisals) and rewards (e.g., bonuses, raises, gifts, approval)—the traditional carrot-and-stick methods. Motivation is seldom about the other person, but more often about *me*. I need to meet my objectives, so I will *motivate* you by offering an incentive (money, a prize, my friendship, approval, etc.) or a punishment (loss of status or job, rejection, disapproval, withholding love, judgement, etc.). Motivation is largely an attempt to alter or control the behavior of others, raise their performance, change attitudes or beliefs or exploit capacity. This is manipulation—Machiavellianism. When we come from this position, we are working principally from our social self and addressing the *social self* of another, tapping into, and exploiting the fears of the person we are trying to motivate, relying on shaming, bribing, rewarding, threatening, or pressuring—all of which trigger our primal fear instincts. When planning an activity, for example, we often ask, "How can I motivate this group to accomplish the tasks I have set for them?"

In a workshop I was running recently, a participant asked me, "The other day, my daughter said she wanted an iPhone. I told her she could have one if she mowed the lawn for the next four weeks. If that is motivation, how should I change so that I inspire her?"

I responded by asking him if he would do this with his spouse. "If your spouse told you that she wanted a new iPhone, would you tell her she could have one if she mowed the lawn for the next four weeks?" He said, "Of course not!" "Why not?" I asked. "Because it is manipulative, insulting and I would get into trouble!" he replied. "Well then," I countered, "why would you do this with your daughter?"

Another motivational technique is to reward or punish an individual with the prospect of being "in" (reward) or "out" (punishment) of favor—("Not only did you forget to mow the lawn, but you are just sulking and behaving like a loser who can't get it together!"). When we use fear, threats, and insults in this way to motivate someone, they will experience anxiety and resentment—they will be uninspired. This is equally true whether we do this to others, or it is done to us.

Our Society is built on the motivational, fear-based, social-self model. Think about marketing: "Buy this lotion or you will be ugly." Our religions are often based on fear: "Join my faith or you will go to hell." Politics run this way, too: "Vote for me or the other guy will raise your taxes." The way we run organizations often falls into this same pattern: "Do what I say, or we'll fire you." And, of course, corporate management has long followed this path: "Achieve these goals, and we will reward you; miss them, and we will punish (or even fire) you." Even some parents use motivation this way: "Do what I say or I'll punish you." Motivation is extrinsic, relies on fear and material rewards or punishments, and is targeted at the level of the social self. Motivation often gets things done—but at a price. And that price is often fear, resentment, anger, lack of trust, and reprisal.

In the short term, motivation works, but it doesn't last, because resentment, exhaustion, and distrust take over. For lasting change, inspiration is the only way.

Inspiration

I do not wish to suggest that motivation is unimportant. If the room you are in catches fire, I will motivate you to get out of it quickly! Instead, what I'm suggesting is that we have become experts at motivation, we have built our societal practices around a fear-based system called motivation, and we have learned to do this extraordinarily well. Our teaching systems, educational facilities, workplaces, laws, and religions are filled with motivation-driven threats, coercions, bribes, bonuses, models, policies, rules, laws, and directives, and, as we all have discovered, they do not always work well. Yet, we have no such equivalent expertise in inspiration. Worse, we use the terms motivation and inspiration interchangeably as if they meant the same thing ("I want to be motivated and inspired!"), and yet, as we are discovering here, motivation and inspiration are almost exact opposites.

Inspiration is intrinsic. Unlike motivation, it does not come from fear, but from love. Unlike motivation, it is not about me—it is almost always exclusively about *you*. Inspiring people—mentors, parents, teachers, and friends and colleagues—want to inspire others to grow, to accomplish *their* objectives, to shine, to reach *their* potential and splendor. Any rewards for people who are inspiring come from the joy they experience when helping others to reach *their* own goals or become larger as fully realized human beings. Therefore, inspiration is an act of love and service to others, whereas motivation is self-centered—Machiavellianistic, narcissistic, and sometimes psychopathic. Like almost everyone, you can likely recall a mentor, teacher, coach, family member, leader, or someone who made a difference in your life—these were all people who *loved* and inspired you. They would not have devoted the time and resources they did to you if they had not felt that way, and to this day, their loving legacy warms your heart. Motivation can be useful sometimes to get small (and occasionally important) things done in the short term; inspiration is more effective in getting big things done over the long term. Inspiration is aimed at the essential self—the soul of another—and is most often generated from within; the inspirer is merely the facilitator of the inspired—this is the essence of a great mentor.

19

As I stated earlier, life is about relationships—with each other, and with everything around us. Every choice we make, and everyone with whom we choose to connect, is the result of our searching for a loving and inspiring relationship. We join companies that inspire us and quit them when they no longer do so. We fall in love with people who inspire us and end the relationship when they no longer do so. We smell a flower, go to a movie, listen to our favorite music, and eat at our favorite restaurants, all because we have a relationship with each of these things, and the people connected to them, that inspire us. When this is no longer true, and we become uninspired, we end the relationship. We pursue inspiring relationships, and we distance ourselves from uninspiring ones. This is the key to our relationships with people. This is true with every relationship in our lives—human and non-human alike—and in every aspect of our lives.

We have become experts at motivation. The playbook for motivation is widely known and practiced—in corporations, families, government, academia, marketing, religions, healthcare, and amongst our friends, but the equivalent playbook for inspiration is far less developed. We now need to become just as effective at inspiring ourselves, inspiring others, and inspiring the world—the Spark, the Flame, and the Torch. When we teach, coach, lead, mentor, or use any other means by which we attempt to enhance and nurture the spirit of another—we will become more effective when we develop inspiring processes and focus on and grow our expertise in inspiring others.

20

How to Distinguish Motivation from Inspiration

- Motivation is based on fear; inspiration is based on love.
- Motivation is based on a need for each other; inspiration is based on love for each other.
- Motivation is driven by the social self; inspiration is energized by the essential self.
- Motivation is based on *me*, on serving my needs; inspiration is based on *you*, on serving *your* needs.
- Motivation is doing something you probably wouldn't do if you didn't have to; inspiration is something you would do anyway.
- Motivation is a "push"; inspiration is a "pull."
- Motivation can be effective for meeting short-term ends; inspiration is more effective for the long term.
- Motivation is an idea you go after; inspiration is an idea that goes after you.

- Motivation is lighting a fire *under* someone; inspiration is lighting a fire *within* someone.

One can see from these distinctions that motivation and inspiration are almost polar opposites. The fact that we use the terms "motivation" and "inspiration" interchangeably suggests that our understanding of the difference is weak, and because of this, we are not clear about when to use the one or the other.

Think of it this way: we hear so frequently that we live in a dangerous world. But could we be overestimating the need to be fearful? Researchers believe that about one percent of the population are psychopaths, and according to the American Psychiatric Association, around 3–5% are sociopaths, while those suffering from antisocial personality disorder, defined as those who consistently disregard and violate the rights of others around them (did you know there was such a thing?) account for about 3–6 percent of the population. Although neither sociopathy nor psychopathy are official diagnostic terms in the Diagnostic and Statistical Manual of Mental Disorders (DSM),[11] and neither map perfectly onto the symptoms of antisocial personality disorder as outlined in the DSM, the constructs are thought to be closely related. So, for argument's sake, let's take an average of 5 percent of the population and assume, these are people who could possibly harm you. That leaves 95 percent of the population who not only pose little or no risk, but may well hold only good intentions for you. For whom will you run your life—the 5 percent or the 95 percent? Motivation runs your life when you bow to the five percent; inspiration runs your life when you relate with and inspire the ninety-five percent.

21

---

11 https://www.psychologytoday.com/us/basics/dsm

It is time to become as expert and practiced at inspiring each other as we have become at motivating each other. Our capacity for relating with others and enhancing their spirit will grow when we develop inspiring processes, make home and work life inspiring, and focus on and grow our practice of being inspiring for others—in every aspect of our lives. We cannot become more inspired, or inspire others, by motivating them.

Maslow and Higher Ground Leadership®

Most people are familiar with Abraham Maslow's five-level Hierarchy of Needs, which he originally proposed in a paper published in 1943 entitled "A Theory of Human Motivation," and later in his 1954 book *Motivation and Personality*. His work is usually interpreted as a pyramid, but Maslow never actually created a pyramid, nor did he say that each level was separate from the others. In his later work, he explored additional aspirations, although these were not part of his original five-level model.

Maslow suggested that all humans follow a linear path that includes several sequential, and incremental, stages from survival to transcendence. This diagram and the descriptions that follow, illustrate the stages of progression:

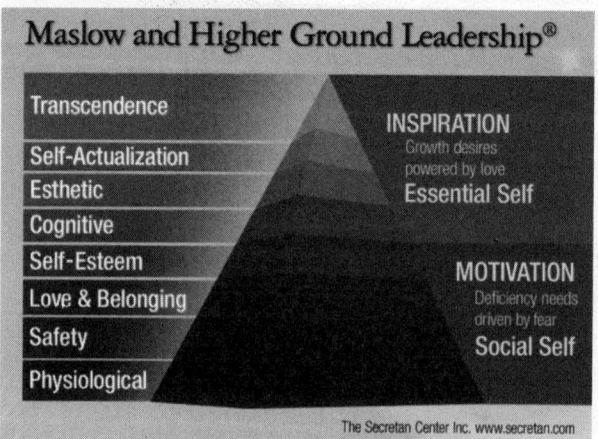

Maslow and Higher Ground Leadership®

Transcendence
Self-Actualization
Esthetic
Cognitive
Self-Esteem
Love & Belonging
Safety
Physiological

INSPIRATION
Growth desires
powered by love
Essential Self

MOTIVATION
Deficiency needs
driven by fear
Social Self

The Secretan Center Inc. www.secretan.com

The Fear-Based Needs:

1. **Physiological Needs**: These include the primal needs of air, water, food, shelter, sex, and other physical needs. Meeting these needs is a prerequisite for progressing to higher needs.

2. **Safety Needs**: If the primal physiological needs are relatively satisfied, the needs that then become dominant arise out of the fear of being unsafe. These needs include health, well-being, and personal and financial safety. Job security also falls within this need category.

3. **Belonging Needs**: When physiological and safety needs are fulfilled, the third priority of human needs becomes social. These belonging needs, which are an interpersonal aspect of Maslow's hierarchy, are motivated by the fear of being deprived of emotionally based relationships, such as with family, friends, and social groups. Failure to meet this need can result in depression, loneliness, and anxiety.

4. **Esteem Needs**: All humans have a need to be respected, valued, and accepted by others. Maslow made a distinction between respect *from* others (a "lower" need) and self-respect (a "higher" need). Deprivation of these needs may lead to an inferiority complex, weakness, and helplessness.

All these first four needs described above are ego-based, emanating from the social self, and **motivated** by a fear of deficiency. At these levels, we are afraid of deficiencies, what we lack in our lives—a scarcity mentality—and fear, as I mentioned earlier, drives motivation.

A shift occurs as we move from fear-based motivations of the first four levels of the hierarchy above to the next four levels, to the aspirational desires. Note that I refer to these as *desires,* not needs, because the former are fear-based, whereas the desires are love-based. As we move from the lower four levels to the higher ones, we move from scarcity thinking to abundance thinking. These are aspirations that we love and that *inspire* us, and they are listed below. We are drawn to the pursuit of personal growth, guiding us toward the aspirational desires we love, and this always emanates from the essential self. *Love generates inspiration.* We love what inspires us.

The Love-Based Desires

While Maslow did not build any additional levels in his original model beyond the fifth one (self-actualization), I describe below an expanded projection of his later work. I am fully aware that I am taking intellectual liberties with my proposition, and I do so with acknowledgment and deference to a brilliant, pioneering thinker.

5. **Cognitive Desires**: Maslow believed that humans have an innate curiosity and a deep desire for personal growth and knowledge. The cognitive desires of the essential self are rooted in a love of the world—curiosity, learning, exploration, discovery, and creativity—all inspiring us to understand. This cognitive desire is characterized by a love of openness to new ideas and concepts (the learner's mindset), a desire to grow, to seek knowledge, learning, and wisdom, and when this is unfulfilled, it can lead to personal frustration and a confused sense of one's place in the bigger scheme of things.

6. **Esthetic Desires**: The essential self seeks beauty over ugliness. We love beauty, harmony, and order, and we love being surrounded by beauty, and when we are, we are inspired. The essential self is nourished in the presence of, and the beauty in, nature, art, and people—infused by the beauty offered by the world. This desire creates a feeling of intimacy with all that is graceful and elegant. This is inspiration.

7. **Self-Actualization Desires**: Maslow clearly described self-actualization as the instinctual desire of humans to realize their full potential. "What a man can be, he must be," Maslow said. This desire, when fulfilled, contributes to the greater good and generates feelings of personal inspiration.

8. **Self-Transcendence Desires**: Maslow believed that the next step for the actualized person was a desire to give themselves to higher goals that transcend the self, relating with others and the world in an altruistic and spiritual way. He wrote, "Transcendence refers to the very highest and most inclusive or holistic levels of human consciousness, behaving and relating, as ends rather than means, to oneself, to significant others, to human beings in general, to other species, to nature, and to the cosmos."[12] For most people, this is not so much a fully realized aspiration, but rather a pilgrimage. It is an inspiring condition of oneness, a deep acceptance of, and love for, the mysteries of the Universe—what some refer to as mysticism.[13]

25

From this description, it can be seen that the first four levels of the hierarchy are needs—not desires—calibrated externally (success), driven by a scarcity outlook and a fear that these needs may not be met. They are rooted in the social self and are highly susceptible to, and likely to generate, fear-based motivation.

As we cross over from the lower four fear-based needs to the higher four love-based desires, things change. We shift from a focus on the social self to a focus on the essential self, from me to you, from

---

12 *Farther Reaches of Human Nature*, Abraham H. Maslow and Bertha G. Maslow, 1993, ISBN-13: 978-0140194708, p. 269.

13 I define a *mystic* as "someone who sees the wonder in everything."

fear to love, from scarcity to abundance, from knowing to learning, and from motivation to inspiration.

We are in a new era in which many of our traditional models and metaphors for managing life have become exhausted and obsolete. Unless we rethink our approach to life and living, we risk alienating an entire generation, who will feel so disenfranchised, and be so disenchanted with the world, that they will despair. We are inadequately prepared if we rely solely on motivation to run our affairs. People are inherently free spirits, and we don't think of work and play as separate domains any more than we separate our work and personal or social life. Everything is connected—it is all one. We need to be inspired. Understanding the power and advantage of inspiration over motivation will bring about a transformation in our appreciation of what our lives and our world could be.[14]

Beyond the Metrics

Even as we are getting richer and richer, we are also getting poorer and poorer. Materially, we have access to more than ever. But spiritually and emotionally, we are struggling. As Mother Teresa portrayed it, "The greatest disease in the West today is not TB or leprosy; it is being unwanted, unloved, and uncared for. We can cure physical diseases with medicine, but the only cure for loneliness, despair, and hopelessness is love. There are many in the world who are dying for a piece of bread, but there are many more dying for a little love. The poverty in the West is a different kind of poverty—it is not only a poverty of loneliness but also one of spirituality. There's a hunger for love, as there is a hunger for God."[15]

---

14 See also the work of Martin Seligman (*Positive Psychology*) and Mihály Csíkszentmihályi (*Flow*).
15 *A Simple Path*, Mother Teresa, Ballantyne Books, 1995

We are in an inspirational void. The pursuit of financial or material rewards alone, and above all else, leads to an imbalance that causes a personal and collective dysfunction. Our social self may be satiated, while our essential self may be bankrupt. How many people do you know, or have read about, who have all the material comforts imaginable, but who are miserable? Our social and corporate cultures have developed into ones that brilliantly reward the metrics of performance while overlooking the measures of the heart, and this has caused an evaporation of inspiration. Leaders, athletes, pop stars, lawyers, movie stars, and other celebrities are remunerated today based on a set of performance metrics that measure material progress but not spiritual or human fulfillment. We measure and reward improvements in share price, return on capital, market share, league standings, wins, box office receipts, and so forth, but not meaning, fulfillment, inspiration, joy, or improvements in the human condition or the health of the planet. In other words, we measure and reward the external, but not the internal—the social self, but not the essential self. And emphasizing the external alone can give us a false sense of happiness—our true joy comes from the internal.

Compared to our conventional metrics, there are no equivalent ones for inspiring and serving customers,[16] creating a loyal and devoted workforce, nurturing their spirit, being kind and sensitive to the environment, honoring our communities and the people who live in them, being caring supporters of the disadvantaged, making the necessary trade-offs and sacrifices and taking the risks that make the world better, or living to more than "the-minimum-required-by-

---

16 Please, let's stop calling human beings "consumers." The term consumer is demeaning and inaccurate, and it separates me from you instead of seeking to make me one with you. I am a person. Please refer to me as a person, and when there are several of us, refer to us as people—and if you must use business jargon, then honor me as a customer or a client.

law" standards of ethics, morals, and values. Even when we do pay attention to these matters, our measurement tools are often poorly calibrated. We reward the creation of wealth, but not stewardship—the outer, but not the inner. There are also natural laws that govern all this: the behavior we reward is encouraged. And we get what we give—*karma*.

And perhaps most importantly, we have forgotten how taking care of each other and our planet is the pinnacle of inspiring behavior—for both those who care and those who are cared for. Indeed, the most effective metric for measuring how well we serve the spirit is the degree to which others find each of us inspiring—as people or organizations.

Meanwhile, the paradox is that as the baby boomers ease into retirement, the next generation is demanding more meaning, fulfillment, compassion, and engagement, causing organization to scramble as they search for relevant new approaches, even as they try to rework centuries-old leadership tools, theories, beliefs, and practices. For all of us today, there seem to be more questions than answers—What is important? What is of value? What adds value? Where do people fit in? What should we trade off? How do we inspire the soul? Is there more than making the numbers each quarter, passing my exam, obtaining a credential?

These are the questions asked by anyone facing a crisis of inspiration.

These are the questions that the following Reflections will seek to answer. And if this book succeeds in igniting a spark within you, then a new flame will begin to burn—*and your life will change.*

The degree to which each of us is inspiring is determined by the degree to which each of us is inspired ourselves. Uninspired people cannot inspire others—it isn't within them. In fact, no one can inspire another person unless they are themselves inspired—parent,

CEO, minister, firefighter, politician, rock star, author—no one. *We experience the world not as it is, but as we are.* Uninspired people find the world uninspiring. Inspired people find the world inspiring and cannot help themselves from inspiring others—it radiates from within them and affects everyone around them, because that is who they are.

How We Misunderstand Leadership

I have spent many years as a practicing leader, including 14 years as a CEO of a *Fortune 200* company. I have written many books about leadership, taught the subject at universities, and coached many leaders worldwide. Along the way, I have learned that leadership is not just about the corporate world, or politics, sports or entertainment. We are all leaders, even when we are in primary school—and all the way to the end of our lives. I have come to the conclusion that leadership, as a discipline or activity, may simply be a subset of something larger—the practice of being an inspiring individual. It is *inspiration* that leads to progress; gets things done; shifts opinions, ideas, and beliefs; creates organizations and grows people; and changes the world. While the process and styles of leadership are important topics, they are far less important than the art of inspiring others. All great leaders are inspiring—but so are great mothers and fathers, siblings, friends, colleagues, and employees. Inspiration is needed by everyone, and everywhere. Inspiration between people depends on a relationship—inspiration cannot occur unless one human being touches the heart of another. Thus leadership in the rather dry, detached, academic form, complete with academic models and theories, as we have come to know it—"old-story" leadership— may run the risk of being uninspiring, especially when it is imperial, hierarchical, mechanical, or theoretical. I do not need a "leader" to lay his or her "new leadership model" on me, and I am sure you don't either. There has been a shocking failure of the "leadership industry" over the last 40 years, even though we spend $170 billion annually on leadership development and there are 240,000 books on leadership available online. All this spending, lecturing, and consulting on leadership has resulted in an inverse correlation—the more we spend, the worse it gets. Although we are all called upon to lead at various times and stages of our lives, it is not "leadership" that we need, but *inspiration*. I will do anything for someone who inspires me. So, the philosophical concept that underpins this book is that if we first become more inspiring as people, we are then able to influence people and the world in an inspiring way—as inspiring fathers and mothers, children, friends, colleagues, pianists, athletes, rock stars, doctors, farmers, or bus drivers, or any other vocation or social role we choose. It's not about leadership—it's about being inspirational—which is a necessary condition of greatness in all things.

Some Simple Steps

We could take this idea further. Suppose that you and I decide that the very first thing we do each day is to make a commitment that all our thoughts, communications, and actions will be inspiring. If we make this simple pledge and then follow through on our intention, our impact on those around us will be remarkable and we will change our lives—and theirs. In fact, one by one, we will change the world. And if a million people took this pledge, we would change the world. Are you prepared to make this commitment? And are you prepared to take action by enrolling your friends and colleagues in this simple endeavor? If you would like to take the pledge to be inspiring for someone in your life today, visit this website to take the first step: www.inspirepledge.com. And if we all choose one person to inspire each day, and add another each following day, we will create a wave that will make a difference.

There are so many simple ways to begin the journey of becoming more inspired, and inspiring. One of my favorites is to use someone's name with them. Suppose we are on a Zoom call together. If I say your name, I guarantee you will smile! Try it. It is a little piece of magic. We are inspired by the sweet sound of our own name.

Here is another idea: suppose you are about to meet with someone whom you find challenging to be with. Before you begin your conversation, repeat these words quietly to yourself, "I love you!" And again, "I love you!" Not out loud, but, quietly, to yourself. The conversation, and your energy that follows, will be transformed. You will be more inspiring for the other person, and the chemistry between you will significantly exceed your expectations. Both of you might even be inspired!

Here is another way to raise you inspiration. Try this: As you begin your day, repeat the mantra "Inspire." The word "inspire" is from the Latin *spirare,* which means *to breathe.* Breathe in the word "Inspire" and take it fully into your entire body. Circulate the energy of inspiration through your heart, pumping the life force of inspiration through your circulatory system to all your organs and every part of your body. Make a commitment to be that word for the rest of the day. Say to yourself, "Inspire! I pledge to be an inspiring person in every thought, word, and deed." Breathe in the awareness of inspiration every chance you get; after all, it's always only a breath away. As you put this declaration into practice, the world will become richer for having experienced you. This is how you can make the difference that you, like all of us, yearn for. The word *conspire* means to breathe together (*con*=with; *spirare*=to breathe); let's breathe together—let's conspire to change the world and make our experience of being alive more inspiring.

My wish for you is that this book will help you to reinvent the way you think about how you relate to others and the world—how inspiring you are. My intention is to be there with you through our dialogue and the exercises and web links are designed to help you to reinvigorate your life, redefine your dreams, and infuse new passion into your very existence. There are many free tools on our website www.secretan.com, and I welcome connections at info@secretan.com.

Lao Tzu said, "It is wisdom to know others; it is enlightenment to know oneself." By reflecting on the concepts presented here, you will be able to redefine the passion within you and how it inspires your life. It will take some effort—some reading, some reflection, and some meditation. But if you invest in and sustain the necessary energy to work through the twelve Reflections in this book, you will discover the *real* reason why you have been put on this Earth, what you have been called to do while you are here, how you will do it, how you will serve, how you will invite others to fully participate with you, how you will nurture and deepen the relationships in your life, how you can live the dream that inspires you, and how you can become more inspired yourself and therefore be an inspiration to others and be an inspiring influence in the world. And knowing this will begin to fill up your reservoirs of inspiration.

This leads to a way of being that is the result of a series of sacred insights, and clarifying those insights is the aim of the first five *Reflections* in this book. How to live in a way that always inspires others, and therefore ourselves, is described in the six Reflections that follow. And how we "pay it forward"[17] is described in the final Reflection.

The aim of this book is ambitious: to help you gain a new and deeper insight into your life and the inspiring role you were born to play; and by so doing, help you to transform yourself first, and as a result, transform everyone else with whom you connect, and to be an inspiration in all other aspects of your life, too. The ambitious journey we are on here together is to reclaim what we have lost—the sense of inspiration we experienced as a child; and to live again—childlike—filled with innocence, not cynicism; with love, not fear; with generosity, not greed; with our spirit guiding us, not our ego—from our essential selves more than our social selves. This book will guide you to work from the inside out rather than the outside in—the opposite approach to almost all contemporary, goal-oriented teaching.

33

....

The Art of Peace begins with you. Work on yourself and your appointed task in the Art of Peace. Everyone has a spirit that can be refined, a body that can be trained in some manner, a suitable path to follow. You are here for no other purpose than to realize your inner divinity and manifest your innate enlightenment. Foster peace in your own life and then apply the Art to all that you encounter.

Morihei Ueshiba

....

---

17 The expression "to pay it forward" describes the concept of generalized reciprocity, in which the recipient of a good deed or favor does a favor to a third party instead of returning the favor..

PART TWO

The Spark—
Inspiring Self

Part Two
The Spark: Inspiring Self

● ● ●

Life begets life. Energy creates energy.
It is by spending oneself that one becomes rich.
—Sarah Bernhardt

Passion and inspiration cannot arise in our lives without the prior ignition of a spark. A spark must be present in order to initiate excitement, passion, a hunger of the spirit, an ambition to accomplish something special, to make a difference. The spark is a sudden awareness, a stirring within, an awakening of our potential, a growing enthusiasm, a realization that we can live large and are capable of changing the world. Without the spark, we are plodding and boring, and our aspirations—both for ourselves and for others—will lack the spiritual oxygen that fuels first the spark, then the flame, and ultimately the torch. This is the listless life that seeps out into the world from us to others, and it is uninspiring—to us and to everyone else, too. The spark ignites the essential self. Thomas Merton said, "Our real journey in life is interior: it is about growth, deepening, and a constant surrender to the deeds of love and grace. This is your calling, and it will bring only joy." And Carl Jung said, "The world will ask you who you are, and if you don't know, the world will tell you." The spark arouses the desire to make a difference, to inspire people, adding electricity, brio, and zest—the stuff that fans the flames of passion and exhilaration within others and brings joy to all. When we light the spark, others experience their lives as being larger, they become more fulfilled, and they feel richer for having experienced us in their lives. This is how the world becomes changed.

Three Big Ideas

The first premise of this book, then, is that all inspired and inspiring people have a deep clarity about three things:

1. Why they are here on Earth
2. What values they will live by, and
3. How they will use their skills and talents to serve the world.

That's it. Simple. But not easy.

Setting Our Intentions

A little appreciated reality is that the majority of people are aching to make a commitment in their lives—to others, to a dream, to the world—if only they could kindle the spark that would lead to action. The two missing links are the belief in oneself and the inspiration we receive from others. Few of us believe that we are rich enough, smart enough, skilled enough, well enough connected, or "lucky" enough to achieve our dreams or effect change. So, we settle for a boring life of mediocrity, and this is uninspiring—not only for us, but also for everyone else with whom we connect.

Let's begin by thinking of ourselves as powerful, translating bold thoughts into bold actions, capable of making change anywhere we wish. The reality is that whatever we do changes the world—we simply need to decide the quality and scale of our purpose in life and therefore how much we will alter the course of the ship we call Earth. Jesus Christ, Mother Teresa, Mahatma Gandhi, Martin Luther King, Jr.—none of these were born with any special privilege. Indeed, they were likely born with less of everything than you and I.

They did not complain—they simply committed to changing the world. Change happens in the world when ordinary people do extraordinary things. This is the opportunity that is open to anybody at any time.

People who are effective (a term we will explore further in Reflection Eleven) inspire others, because it is inspiring to see people actually getting things done rather than merely talking about them. And the act of being effective is inspiring because we are a species that seeks completion and order. Loose ends and untidiness frustrate; conclusions and closures offer a sense of satisfaction and tidiness—an inner pleasure that flows from the completion of tasks, projects, or missions. The experience of effectiveness is intensely satisfying and inspiring.

The Power of Inspiration

How might the world look if we became *fully conscious,* inviting the essential self—the inspirer that resides within—to upgrade our previously learned behaviors? The result would be a life lived as a person who inspires others and as a person who, therefore, is inspired by others. We are all capable of achieving this state—but it requires our conscious and ongoing commitment to achieve its full expression. Let's begin by describing how we experience a person whose energy comes from their essential self. Inspiring people always lift the spirits of others.

Inspirational relationships with others require us to fall in love with the process of inspiring others and connecting them with passion and joy, continuously—to paraphrase St. Thomas Aquinas— *willing, and actively supporting, the good of the other.* Inspiring relationships are not a formula or a model. Nor are they a "system" or a "process" that can be copied without connection to the heart.

Inspiration is a way of *being*. And when we are inspiring, inspiration flows from our essential self—from our heart to the heart of another.

Thus, we can be inspired by a beautiful flower—because it lifts our spirit. Or by another person, because they lift our spirit. Whenever we are inspired, it is because someone, or something, has lifted our spirit—they are sharing their love from their essential self to ours.

When we use the term "leader," it is meant to be synonymous with parent, teacher, executive, minister, politician, counselor, friend, son or daughter, husband or wife—even simply with "human being." This is because we are *all* leaders. This is why I use the term "leadership" in such an all-inclusive way. We are all called to lead in almost every aspect and stage of our lives, and inspiring leadership is an essential ingredient of every part of life. Inspirational leadership builds relationships, forms friendships, changes thinking and philosophies, gives birth to new ideas, and shapes lives and hearts. As children, we are leaders—at school, in sports, in our pastimes, and in our friendships. As we grow and become parents, we are invited to assume new leadership responsibilities. We are called to lead at home, in our places of worship, in our corporations, in our communities, and in our countries. Inspirational leadership changes the world. But leadership is not a "technique" or a subject we learn in a seminar or from a book, because it is not a "method"—it is an emotional connection, a way of life, and a way of being with others. It is not traditional textbook leadership we are looking for, but inspiration.

The kind of leadership we are describing here—personal and inspirational leadership—is an inside job, and when awareness of this is weak, it is uninspiring, but once this awareness is strong, great personal leadership can be lived. Inspirational leadership flows from the essential self and elevates the essential selves of others.

Destiny, Character, and Calling:
Our Why-Be-Do®

It is strange that we should attempt to live with only the acquired superficiality of "living skills" that are principally found in our social self, our personality. And it is equally strange—and even unnerving—that we are prepared to live with the sadness that results when we allow the precious gifts of our essential self to die inside us while we are living, for a life that only reflects the social self is a life that fails to inspire. The social self tends to spend money we do not have, on stuff we do not need, to impress people who merely judge us superficially. How might we touch the world if we became fully conscious, totally awake and aware of our Destiny, Character, and Calling—our North Star, our sacred purpose for being here in *this* moment in space and time, with the full awareness that we are all one?

How did we forget who we are? And, having forgotten, how and why have we let *others* define for us who we are? Why have we handed over our power to others—authority figures, thought leaders, social norms, media stereotypes, or what our parents and teachers told us we needed to be? As a result of all this social programming, our social self rules our life, constantly calibrating externally, looking for "success" instead of joy, and endlessly seeking external approval. This is a recipe for failure as we will never meet the expectations others constantly demand of us. Surely, we are the best suited to make our own discoveries—with the counsel of others, of course. But our own North Star must be the final arbiter. In his 2005 Stanford commencement address, Steve Jobs said, "Your time is limited, so don't waste it living someone else's life. Don't be trapped by dogma—which is living with the results of other people's thinking. Don't let the noise of other's opinions drown out your own inner voice". And Oscar Wilde said, "Be yourself; everyone else is taken." Our essence is the source of our unique authenticity and integrity. And where will we find the answers? As we all know but seldom acknowledge, the answers lie within. As Sri Ramana Maharshi put it, "Happiness is your nature. It is not wrong to desire it. What is wrong is seeking it outside when it is inside." Of course, this does not mean to imply that the singular pursuit of happiness is the end game, either—as Viktor Frankl, psychiatrist and Auschwitz survivor, wrote in the classic, *Man's Search for Meaning*, "...a human being is not one in pursuit of happiness but rather in search of a reason to become happy..." This, as we shall see, is a very important distinction.

Few of us have thought about why we have been placed on this Earth—our *reason* to become happy—and, if we were asked this question, we might become strangely tongue-tied. But how can we be inspired and inspire others if we cannot even explain the reason for our own existence in the first place—the reason why we are here? Life is not the practice of manipulating, motivating, and controlling the behavior of others in order to achieve what we want. That is a behavior that emanates from the social self. Inspiring others is achieved when we practice being an inspiration to others by drawing from our inner, authentic selves—emanating from the essential self. Relating with other souls is not so much something we learn; it is more something we *live*. We cannot "do" relationships—it is something we express through *being*. We don't "do" relationships—we *feel* them. To quote Saint Francis of Assisi, "Preach the gospel at all times, and if necessary, use words."

If we have no idea about what we are supposed to be doing while we are on this planet, then we cannot know the practical purpose and sacred intent of our lives, and our relationships will be lived from an empty place. Therefore, whatever the form of living we practice, it will have no spiritual brilliance—the spark, the inspiration—to ignite the flame and then shine on the path that advances or justifies our life's purpose. As the Buddha said, "Just as a candle cannot burn without fire, men cannot live without a spiritual life."

Søren Kierkegaard, the great Danish philosopher, asked,

> "One sticks one's finger into the soil to tell by the smell in what land one is: I stick my finger in existence—it smells of nothing. Where am I? Who am I? How came I here? What is this thing called the world? What does this world mean? Who is it that has lured me into the world? Why was I not consulted, why not made acquainted with its manners and customs instead of throwing me into the ranks, as if I had been bought by a kidnapper, a dealer in souls? How did I obtain an interest in this big enterprise they call reality? Why should I have an interest in it? Is it not a voluntary concern? And if I am to be compelled to take part in it, where is the director? I should like to make a remark to him. Is there no director? Whither shall I turn with my complaint?"

At an instinctive level, we are all full of questions about our existence, but we choose to put them in a little black box while we busy ourselves with the mundane or reference our lives against external criteria—thus living from our social selves and ignoring our essential selves.

As W. H. Auden sardonically put it, "We are here on earth to do good for others. What the others are here for, I don't know." Of course, he had his tongue in his cheek, for he surely knew that others were here for the same purpose as he.

How can we know that our efforts are relevant to the purpose of our lives—to do good for others—to serve others? Surely the things we do on a day-to-day basis should lead to something meaningful, should serve others more than ourselves, and should come from the most authentic part of our being. Whatever we do should amount to something, lead to something, change something, and make something better.

Without a sense of connection to a divine purpose or higher power, we will default into "autopilot," practicing a way of being that we may have learned by reading an autobiography or by watching a film and copying our TV heroes and influencers. I am sure you know many people who live their rudderless lives this way. Or we may measure our effectiveness by referencing metrics that satisfy the social self but leave the essential self gasping for spiritual oxygen. We need a deeper sense of who we are, and an acceptable and uplifting balance between our social self and our essential self, following our North Star, to be fully present as conscious beings, before we can presume to inspire others.

So often, our social self controls our behavior, which leads to much affectation—we learn "techniques" and "the tricks of the trade"— how to dress, what to say, how to make a speech, how to command attention, how to behave in a meeting, how to persuade others, how to make small talk, how to charm, how to climb the corporate ladder, how to be politically correct, and an endless array of other superficialities. Through all this, the essential self waits patiently while the personality asserts and indulges itself in its shallow journey. This unconscious way of living is self-serving—dominated by the social self instead of being the result of a powerful, integrity-centered passion, and it is, therefore, uninspiring. The truth is, nothing commendable happens on Earth without the presence of inspiration. But because the essential self sits patiently in the shadow of the social self, it often remains unheard—suspended. Meanwhile, the social self engages in *doing* instead of *being*. For many inspiring people, the essential self has been awakened by a growing awareness of its long-silenced voice and so their life's journey is guided by respecting and listening to it.

This is the difference between sleep-walking through our lives and becoming awake—the difference between being a slave of the social self instead of aligning the social self and the essential self to make an inspiring life, a whole, integrated life—the difference between doing and being, the difference between being unconscious and becoming conscious, the difference between carrot-and-stick methods and inspiring people. It is the difference between talking about inspiration and being inspiring. In order to engage the essential self, we must ask questions that go beyond the social self, such as, "What am I communicating when I am not speaking?" "What am I teaching when I am simply being"? "How can I serve?" "How can I make the world a better place?" And we must be rigorously objective with the answers we hear in response to these questions, and then ask if we are satisfied with them. Asking subtle questions from the purity of the essential self like these is a sign that the inspiring being within us has been awakened, is becoming conscious, and is getting ready to become inspired and be inspiring for others from a place of inner wisdom, authenticity, and integrity, rather than from a superficial, parroted approach that lacks substance and roots. And it is a sign that we have become open, because ears already filled with answers cannot hear. As Rabbi Zusya so eloquently put it, "In the world to come, I shall not be asked, "Why were you not Moses?" I shall be asked, "Why were you not Zusya?"

And Sri Ramana Maharshi explains, "Nearly all mankind is more

45

or less unhappy because nearly all do not know the true Self. Real happiness abides in Self-knowledge alone. All else is fleeting. To know one's Self is to be blissful always."

This is the journey we will now begin—the discovery of self, the journey that will inspire you, and therefore inspire others—the journey that adds inner metrics to the outer ones.

....

"Come to the edge," he said.
"We can't, we're afraid!" they responded.
"Come to the edge," he said.
"We can't, we will fall!" they responded.
"Come to the edge," he said.
And so they came.
And he pushed them.
And they flew.

Guillaume Apollinaire

Reflection One:
DESTINY

*When you are inspired by some great purpose, some
extraordinary project, all your thoughts break their bonds;
your mind transcends limitations, your consciousness expands
in every direction, and you find yourself in a new, great and
wonderful world. Dormant forces, faculties and talents become
alive, and you discover yourself to be a greater person by
far than you ever dreamed yourself to be.*
—Patanjali

Your North Star

We often use the metaphor of the *North Star* and there is a historical reason for this. Because the star Polaris, generally called the North Star, shines directly onto Earth's North Pole, it has been used for centuries by navigators as a guide when plotting a route in the northern hemisphere. The same star is used as a navigational aid by many species of birds, as well as by salmon, dolphins, and whales. The North Star represents a fixed bearing in the sky which enables the traveler to plot a route and stay on course. It has helped millions over time, to stay on a path to their desired destination.

During the early period of American history, when slavery was prevalent, slaves seeking freedom from captivity knew it was unsafe to escape in daylight, so they traveled by night. Having no signposts or visible landmarks, they followed the North Star, because they knew it would guide them to freedom. The slaves passed a song among themselves that contained the coded directions for traveling north. It was called "Follow the Drinking Gourd." The "Drinking Gourd" refers to a hollowed-out gourd, which was frequently used by slaves and other rural Americans as a water dipper. It represented a code for the star formation of the Big Dipper, which points directly to the North Star.

These freedom seekers knew that if they kept the North Star firmly in their sights, and remained centered on it, they would never be lost. And so it is for you.

What is your North Star? What is your path to inner freedom? What is the internal power that provides the strength of focus and clarity in your life? What inspires you; what is the spark that lights your fire and keeps you directed? When you discover it, it will be the spark that begins the process of helping you to feel alive. This spark is ignited when you become aware of the deep passion residing in your Destiny, Character, and Calling. The spark is your inner knowing that, when it is revealed, is so certain, secure, and keen, that it steers you towards your life's purpose—your reason for being. The spark is the radiance within you that ignites your passion and inspiration and makes you an inspiring being.

Passion Is the Authentic Guide for Our Choices

A common characteristic of inspired people is the spark that becomes their North Star—they have absolute clarity about who they are and what they want to do with their lives—so much clarity, in fact, that it radiates a vibrant energy that others feel and experience, and it inspires everyone. Reflect on this a minute: People who, to most of us, would seem to be disadvantaged, or impaired in some way, suddenly take on the capacity to achieve great feats, to excel beyond the ordinary, to accomplish the remarkable, because of the pull of their focus. Their North Star is so powerful, it shines brighter than any other and speaks directly to them. When we have this clear inner knowing, all obstacles—even extreme physical limitations or adverse business conditions—become inconsequential. Sarah Reinertsen, for instance, shrugged off adversity, becoming the first female amputee to compete in and conquer the Ford Ironman Triathlon Kona (a 2.4-mile swim, 112-mile bike ride, and 26.2-mile run)—an astounding feat. "My dream is to do extraordinary things every day," she says. Kyle Maynard, who suffers from a congenital defect that robbed him of his arms from above the elbows and his legs from above the knees, follows the motto, "It's not what I can do, but what I will do." That is the attitude that has spurred him to become a winning high-school wrestler, weightlifter, and gifted student—and now an entrepreneur, speaker, and best-selling author, and an inspiration to everyone who knows him.

Creating a Destiny Statement

I and my colleagues have conducted hundreds of workshops in which participants have discovered their Destiny, and it is enormously gratifying to watch the self-discovery and liberation that are released when that spark is ignited by the newly revealed passion that has lain dormant for years within many of the participants. One woman said that apart from giving birth to her daughter, this was the most exciting experience of her entire life!

How do we define a Destiny Statement?

Here is a simple but profound process to help you unfold this for yourself. (There is a free worksheet available for you to use as you define your Why-Be-Do® here: https://secretan.com/Why-Be-Do-Worksheet.pdf). What excites you? You may find this process to be paradoxical, but stay with me here—you will be surprised by what you discover:

There are two givens that we all share:

1. Our passion is drawn to the things that excite us—positively (the light) *and* negatively (the shadow); and

2. At our core, we all yearn to serve and improve the world.

Very often it is the shadow just as much as the light that engages us. We are animated by what inspires us just as much as by what repulses or shocks us. Carl Jung reminds us that "One finds one's destiny on the path one takes to avoid it." In the spaces below, write down one or two things that you feel are *wrong* with the world—we will call these *Terrathreats*—the shadows of the world. These are issues that you consider to be so serious that unless they are resolved, they will be radically detrimental to the world and might even cause the demise of humanity and the Earth. What are the challenges facing the world, in your opinion, that have the potential to destroy life, or humanity, or Earth? This is a deeply personal question—it is not about what others think, but about what troubles *you* and concerns *you* most about the world.

One more thing before you begin to write: You may be thinking, "Oh, I'm just little ole' me–I can't change the world." But reflect on Bernard Shaw's words:

> This is the true joy in life: Being used for a purpose recognized by yourself as a mighty one, being a force of nature instead of a feverish, selfish little clod of ailments and grievances, complaining that the world will not devote itself to making you happy. I am of the opinion that my life belongs to the whole community and as long as I live, it is my privilege to do for it what I can. It is a sort of splendid torch which I have got hold of for the moment, and I want to make it burn as brightly as possible before handing it on to future generations.

As I observed earlier, many people who changed the world came from very humble beginnings—Jesus Christ, Mahatma Gandhi, Martin Luther King, Jr., Nelson Mandela, Mother Teresa—none of these were privileged or powerful, they simply had a burning inner passion, "a splendid torch," as Bernard Shaw put it. They had a spark—a North Star—to address the wrongs of the world. So why not you? You are starting with even greater advantages than they had.

I will use my own example as a guide for you so you can follow the same process for creating your own Destiny Statement:

A *Terrathreat* is a blight, a cancer, an extreme danger to the world, that could easily destroy our lives, or our planet, if it were not contained. In my case, I feel that violence is a continuum, which, if it grows, can be terminal—from trivial abuses to genocide and war, and everything in between. According to Comscore, over the last decade, PG-13 movies have grossed $54.6 billion, PG movies earned $24.3 billion, R movies, $26.5 billion, and G movies, $2.7 billion. So, I wonder, are we addicted to violence? Or does our media manipulate us and cause the addiction? Can we make alternative choices, and if we did, would we change the world? Would humanity evolve if we chose love over fear and violence? These are some of the questions behind my first Terrathreat. I have another: I believe that the way we are exhausting and polluting our planet is unsustainable (science writer Tim De Chant has suggested that we would need 3.9 Earths to sustain the world's population at American levels[18]). So, my second Terrathreat is "degradation." My Terrathreats, then, are *violence* and *degradation.* As you can probably tell, these are issues about which I feel deeply passionate.

51

---

18 https://www.bbc.com/news/magazine-33133712

In the spaces below, write down one (or at most two) thing(s) that you deem to be potentially catastrophic threats to the world—your Terrathreats—and that hold the possibility of threatening or mortally wounding the world, and to cause serious global damage if we don't change, arrest, or reverse them. These are dangerous challenges that arouse your own passion and about which you hold grave concerns. Use just one word, not a phrase, to describe the Terrathreat:

My Terrathreat(s) is (are):

1. _____

2. _____

The Terrathreats about which you feel deeply concerned, represent the shadow within you, the aspects of yourself, and your inner world, that trouble you and which you may try to avoid. But embracing our shadow is the ultimate act of self-love which can lead to breakthroughs and transformational change. History has many examples of great manifestos being written in the reverse—bringing the shadow into the light. For example, "No taxation without representation" is a political slogan that originated in the American Revolution, and which expressed one of the primary grievances of the American colonists against Great Britain. Its opposite became part of the American Declaration of Independence—"For imposing taxes on us without our consent"—and as a result, changed the course of history.

Therefore, if the Terrathreat is the path to ruin for the world, what would the opposite look like? What is the antonym? For example, if *scarcity* were your Terrathreat, an antonym might be *abun-*

dance. Using my own example again, my Terrathreats are *violence* and *degradation*. The antonyms (as I interpret them, at least) are *love* and *sustainability*, respectively.

Now write the antonym(s) of your Terrathreat(s)—what we call the *Terrafix(es)*—the exact opposite(s) of the words you used for your Terrathreat(s)—in the spaces below. A Terrafix should not be an interpretation or paraphrasing, but the *exact* opposite word—the antonym. For example, the opposite of *fear* might be *love*, or of *ignorance* could be *learning*, and so on. Use a thesaurus if you find it helpful. Write each Terrafix below with just one word:

My Terrafix(es) is (are):

1. _____

2. _____

The next step is to craft these two Terrafix words into a sentence that will be your Destiny Statement. Using my own example, I took the two Terrathreats—violence and degradation—and determined that their antonyms were *love* and *sustainability,* and I wove these two Terrafixes into this Destiny Statement:

I am Lance Secretan. My Destiny Statement is:
*To create a more **loving** and **sustainable** planet.*

See how this works? Here is another example: Deanna Stull is the Chief Experience Officer of CoachVille Inc., and a senior member of our teaching faculty at the Secretan Center. She believes that alienation and loneliness are dangerous for civilization and that we need to help those who feel alienated or lonely, in order to avoid a societal catastrophe. She chose *belonging* as the antonym of *Alienation* so *belonging* became her Terrafix. Weaving this into a Destiny Statement, Deanna created this:

I am Deanna Stull. My Destiny Statement is:
To create a sense of profound belonging for everyone.

Here are a few more examples to inspire your creative juices and for you to use as a model—note the brevity:

I am Steve Hultquist (Personal and Leadership Coach).
My Destiny Statement is:
To generate greater love and awareness.

I am Wally Amos
(Inventor of Famous Amos Chocolate Chip Cookies).
My Destiny Statement is: *To elevate self-esteem in society.*

I am Ed Boudreau, MD (*Emergency physician*).
My Destiny Statement is: *To make the world simpler.*

There are further resources for you on the Why-Be-Do® Forum, where many people have posted their Destiny, Character and Calling Statements—their Why-Be-Do® statements—which you may find helpful. Remember, plagiarism is encouraged—there are only a few ways in which we can describe how we will change the world, and if someone has used words that resonate with you, please use them. That is the purpose of the Why-Be-Do® Forum which you can find here: https://secretan.com/tools/forums/why-be-do_forum/

Before you write your Destiny Statement, take a look at this 2½-minute video, "A Divine Conversation," that we have created for you: https://secretan.com/adivineconversation/. Now craft your one (or two, if you prefer, but no more) *Terrafix* words into a sentence that describes how you wish to dedicate your life.

Write yours:

My Destiny Statement is:

_____

_____

Reflect on this for a moment. Are you prepared to live your life in service of this Destiny Statement? Marvel at these words! Friedrich Nietzsche said, "He who has a why to live for can bear almost any how."

You have created an awesome thing—a definition of the reason why you are here on this planet, and how you plan to live your life from here on in. This is the ignition of your spark. It will light your fire. Few people arrive at this clarity at any time in their lives. Savor the inspiration, the liberation, and the centering feeling it offers you. Celebrate it privately first, and when you are ready, share it with your loved ones. Then celebrate it with everyone you trust and those whom you wish to inspire. When you feel comfortable doing so, share it with your colleagues and those whom you lead, teach, and coach—they will be inspired by your Destiny Statement. Explain to them that this is why you are here on Earth, this is why and how you lead, how you live your life, this is your essential self revealed—this is who you are. Eventually, when you are ready, and as you hone and polish your Destiny Statement, share it with the world—even on your business cards and your email signature.[19]

---

19 Submit your own Why-Be-Do Statement and draw inspiration from reading those of many others at https://secretan.com/tools/forums/why-be-do_forum/

Over the next few months, these words—so vital to the future of your life, and therefore the quality of your life—will fit increasingly snugly with your essential self. Perhaps you may find a word a little awkward here and there, and you may need to "tweak" some of the language and make it a perfect fit for you—this is normal because this is a continuous process. This is something that perhaps you have never done in your life before, and now you have created a clear definition of why you are here on this planet in less than a day! It may evolve, and be burnished over time, but the core idea of your Destiny has now been revealed!

....

Resolve to be thyself;
and know, that he who finds himself,
loses his misery.
Matthew Arnold

....

Reflection Two:
CHARACTER

Be more concerned with your character than your reputation,
because your character is what you really are, while your
reputation is merely what others think you are.
—John Wooden

Courage. Kindness. Friendship. Character.
These are the qualities that define us as human beings,
and propel us, on occasion, to greatness.
—R. J. Palacio, "Wonder"

In the last Reflection, you accomplished something very few people ever do in their entire lives—you developed clarity about your life's Destiny—*why* you are here on this Earth. This is the first step in igniting the spark that will excite and inspire you, and this energy will transmit to others—your inspiration will radiate from within you to others. Many people have developed mission statements or can recite a homily about their life goals: to retire by 50, to provide for their children, to run a big company, to contribute to their community. These are all noble and worthy goals, but mission statements are an outdated methodology that served an old paradigm of goal-oriented, materially-based objectives. Understanding and following our Destiny, on the other hand, enables us to reach for more than mere targets of material success and objectives driven by the social self—it connects us to the energy of the entire universe, expressed as the inner wisdom that directs our individual and collective lives, reaching for something greater than our own secular ambitions.

Character and How We Serve

One of the great gifts that come with knowing one's Destiny is the awareness that we are here to serve. Paul said we should "serve one another in love" (Galatians 5:13). And Sri Sathya Sai Baba said, "Serve man until you see God in all men." It is by serving each other that we serve a higher power and become inspiring. All major philosophies and religions support this concept, which is also an ideal to which effective societies and organizations aspire.[20] So, if our highest purpose while we are here on Earth is to serve each other, and therefore a higher purpose than just ourselves, how are we to do this, and how can we determine our own unique Character that will enable us to do so in a way that inspires—us and others?

We serve each other, and the larger collective—Earth, the universe, the Creator—not through the *doing* that is described in so much of our goal-oriented literature and teaching, but more through the *being: who* we are; not through our accomplishments, but through our presence; not from our social self, but through our essential self; not through our success, but through our integrity and joy; not just through the force of our personality, but through the radiance of our essential self. Character is how we choose to *be*—particularly when we think no one is looking. As Dwight L. Moody once remarked, "Character is what you are in the dark."

So, our Character describes the way we want to be in the world, the ways in which we wish to touch others' lives and set an example. It describes how we want to be remembered—our moral legacy. Abraham Lincoln put it this way: "Character is like a tree and repu-

---

20 The concept of service is discussed in greater detail in Reflection Eight.

tation like its shadow. The shadow is what we think of it; the tree is the real thing." How will your tree grow, and what shadow will it cast? Think of it as your personal "brand." If people were to describe you, what would they say about you? Would their description be the same as the way you would like to be known? And if so, what would that be?

When considering the attributes of people who are motivating, those that belong to the social self are numerous and quickly come to mind—ambitious, visionary, focused, determined, strong, powerful, dominant, motivational—to name a few. But we rarely connect at a soulful level with these aspects in those who attempt to motivate us because these are characteristics of the social self. We are more likely to be inspired (not motivated) by characteristics found in the essential self—love, inspiration, fun, joy, creativity, compassion, empathy, vulnerability, humility, generosity, and more. To the untrained or unconscious ear, these may be considered by some as "weak," "soft," or "fluffy," but to the inspired and the inspiring, they are the opposite. Remember the Iroquois saying, "It takes a strong man to be gentle." Our greatest strengths are the qualities that make us human and *real*.

Merriam-Webster defines Character as "one of the attributes or features that make up and distinguish an individual; the complex of mental and ethical traits marking and often individualizing a person, group, or nation; main or essential nature." Theodore Roosevelt described it this way: "Character, in the long run, is the decisive factor in the life of an individual and of nations alike." Our Character Statement describes how we want to *be* in the world—how we want to *live* to make a difference, how we can be most effective in relating with others and the world, how we make the world better, how we become more inspiring, to ourselves and to others, as much of the

59

time as possible—and on really good days, even a bit more! Note the emphasis on *living* our Character—as Thomas Payne wrote: "Reputation is what men and women think of us; character is what God and angels know of us."

When our time comes, we leave behind our fame and material possessions, but we take our Character with us, because it is how we will be remembered.

Defining a Character Statement

Our task, then, is to craft a clear definition of how we want to *be* on this planet—the *BE* of our Why-Be-Do®—our Character Statement—that describes how we will *be* as we serve and fulfill our Destiny. It describes how we would like others to know us—when we are functioning as the best version of ourselves. Let's walk through the process together for creating a Character Statement, and I will use my own example as a model:

At times, I can be judgmental. I have opinions about everything from how toothpaste should be squeezed out of the tube to how the judges should vote on *American Idol* and how the President of the United States should run the country and interact with the world. Note the overuse of the word "should." In my private moments, I even have opinions about what God should do to improve the world! These judgments—which, of course, come straight from my social self—can easily slip into "right" and "wrong" statements, making some people "good" and others "bad." Of course, this is not always the most endearing or productive practice, and it sometimes damages relationships because it creates separateness, not oneness—judgment is a weapon that divides. At its worst, it alienates people, and at its best, it helps me to learn that others experience it as uninspiring and unloving.

Notice that this is another example of reaching into our shadow for answers. What I learn from doing so is that being a judgmental or critical person does not come across to others as a loving way to be, regardless of my intentions. In my role as a leader, parent, or friend, I have found that if I want to guide the behavior of others, or if I wish to inspire a team into action or to follow a strategy, I must first love them—and be sure my actions show that I love them—and from this loving place, I am then more able to inspire them. As a spouse, if I wish to build a solid, lifelong relationship with my partner, I must love her and inspire her every day. As a father, if I want the best for my children, I must love them and be an inspiring influence for them. As a friend, I must love the other and be so inspiring that they seek my company. If I want to change the world, I need to love others so much that they are inspired to change the world, to work for the greater good, and to achieve something of significance. That's what I know, but it isn't always the way I live!

Reflecting on what I do that gets in my own way and diminishes the level of fulfillment and meaning I achieve in my life leads to a greater awareness of how I *need* to be. Or, to put it more positively, it informs me about how I will choose to live my life—how I *will* be— so that it contributes to the kind of world I long for. I realize that I will not attain a perfect state in this aspiration, but, most days, I try my best. My personal discovery, then, is that I can be most effective in the world if, and when, I am a loving and inspiring person. So, this reveals the Character traits I want to embody—the definition of how I wish to *be*—and so I choose:

My Character Statement is:

To be an inspiring and loving person

This, then, becomes my Character Statement. How can I seriously expect to influence others or have an inspiring relationship with
them from any place that is fear-based, motivational, negative, coercive, sarcastic, manipulative, diminishing, selfish, political, pressuring, authoritarian, pushy, aggressive, ambitious, dishonest, nag-
ging, browbeating, blustering, or dominating? These are all "push"
behaviors, coming from the social self, so frequently used in our
society and in our motivational theories.

But the more I push, the more I invoke Newton's Third Law of
Mechanics: *Every action has an equal and opposite reaction.* Therefore, the more I push, the more I will be *pushed back*. On the other
hand, the more I am open—that is, *loving*—the more I invoke "pull"
energy, the more I will inspire others to the common good, and,
using the same Law of Mechanics, the more I will attract reciprocal energy. So, if my Character invokes advantages for the common
good—if I am loving and inspiring—I will attract others to join
me on the same path. This is how we become inspiring and inspire
others. It is the art of getting things accomplished in our own lives
and the lives of others—through them—by loving and inspiring
them—in order to be a positive influence on the world. I write all
this with the sure knowledge that this is an *aspiration* for me—not
something I have fully accomplished, lest you should think I have
this all buttoned up in my life!

Defining Your Own Character Statement

What is your Character Statement? How do you wish to "be" in
this life? How will you live in order to inspire yourself and therefore
others? How do you wish others to know you? What words would
you like to have inscribed on your tombstone?

Here are a few examples to inspire your creative juices and for you to use as a model—again, note the brevity:

Arnie Wohlgemut
(Consultant, and Higher Ground Leadership® Pathfinder).
My Character Statement is: *To be a passionate and kind person.*

Scott Regan
(Strategy and Marketing Consultant,
and Higher Ground Leadership® Pathfinder).
My Character Statement is:
To be an authentic, inspiring, and uplifting person.

Colin Platt (Vice President, Aon PLC (Canada),
and Higher Ground Leadership® Pathfinder).
My Character Statement is:
To be loving, inspiring, empathetic, and enthusiastic.

Rob Ryder
(former Vice President of Learning and
Leadership Development, Centura Health).
My Character Statement is:
To touch hearts and inspire souls with beauty and wisdom.

Rob Ryder, whose Character Statement is shown above, says, "I refer to this statement constantly, both in public and for myself. It defines my life, not just my work, and I find comfort in having it as a compass as I plot my course through whatever life happens to be throwing at me in any given moment. In many ways, it is an affirmation of what I am and what I aspire to. I have not changed it at all since getting comfortable with it nine years ago."

Our Character Statement, as well as our Destiny and Calling Statements, may evolve over time and require refinement or revisions. For example, Sister Nancy Hoffman, former vice president of Mission, Centura Health, in Colorado, originally formulated her Character statement as follows:

To strive to act justly and love tenderly in all situations

Sometime later, she revised it to:

To act justly and love tenderly in all situations

Notice the elimination of the words "to strive." Sister Nancy Hoffman explains, "I have become very intentional and focused in my life, using my Destiny, Character, and Calling (Why-Be-Do®) as a guide to how I wish to *be* in this world of form. I wish to *be* God's unconditional love for all of creation, I wish to *be* peace, I wish to *be* just, and I wish to *be* love. No more trying or striving, just present-moment *being.* Sound too radical and/or Eastern for a Catholic nun? So be it!"

Now write your own Character Statement—how do you want to *be* in this world? How do you wish to live your life? What qualities do you want to live by so that they are an inspiring beacon and model for others? How will you *be* so that others will look to you as their role model, the epitome of what they wish to become? How do you want to be remembered at the end of your life—how do you hope others will describe your character?

One more thing: be brief—six to eight words or less. You may think that it can't be done but remember that Ernest Hemingway once wrote a story in just six words—"For sale: baby shoes, never worn."—and he is said to have called it his best work!

Now write yours:

My Character Statement is:

_____

_____

Reflection Three:
CALLING

Your profession is not what brings home your paycheck.
Your profession is what you were put on earth to do. With such
passion and such intensity that it becomes spiritual in calling.
—Vincent Van Gogh

Many people work just to make a living—only an inspired minority are living fully because they *love* their work. In my research, 80 percent of those surveyed say they would give up their day jobs if they had a free choice. This demonstrates a depressing mismatch between what people feel called to do, and what they actually end up doing.

A Calling is the pursuit of a vocation—from the Latin *vocare*: to call—that inspires; it is living a dream; it is the experience of radiant relevance. It is doing the work you love, something that you would do anyway.

Recently, I was working with a local community that had asked me to help them become a world-class center for entrepreneurs and technology experts. They wanted to be a magnet for cutting-edge thinkers and creative entrepreneurs who lived elsewhere but would relocate to their community, thus helping them to become a center of innovation and excellence. During our sessions, I invited them to develop a clear definition of why they existed, how they would be, and how they would use their gifts to serve—their Destiny, Character, and Calling Statements. This enabled each of them to describe their uniqueness and helped them to contribute to the building of an international reputation for their community that would attract the talent they sought. In the course of my work with them, each of the

400 leaders participating in the conference was able to develop their own personal Destiny, Character, and Calling Statements to ensure that there was a tight alignment between their own personal dreams and aspirations and those of their community. This is how teams are guided to greatness. (The importance of having a single dream is discussed in Reflection Five.)

One of the participants, Leo Deveau, was struggling. He was a market researcher, but he had not yet found his true Calling. I asked him where his passion lay, and after some hesitation, in which he seemed to fumble for an appropriate "business" response, he described his love of music. During our lunch break, some of the participants took me aside to explain that this man was a brilliant musician. So, I asked Leo if he would like to play for the audience at the end of our meal and, reluctantly, he agreed. Since we were in a theater, I reasoned that we might find a piano somewhere, and we did, and with the help of two stagehands, we lugged it into the lunch area.

After lunch, Leo sat down at the piano—and he let it rip! For a moment it seemed as though Jerry Lee Lewis had just set fire to the piano. Leo raised the roof! Everyone could sense that he had come alive—this was a moment of pure joy for him as he rocked the room—this market researcher had morphed into a rock star! The audience erupted into a dancing, clapping, and whistling frenzy—a sea of inspired grins.

Leo ended his virtuoso performance with a flourish, and I thanked him. As the lengthy applause subsided, we all returned to the auditorium to continue our meeting. Before we began, I asked the audience, "Can anyone help Leo define his true Calling?" and they erupted into cheers, chanting, "Music! Music! Music!" Then I turned to Leo and said, "Are you still unclear about your Calling?"

Sometime later, Leo told me, "This experience enabled me to recognize and honor the God-given talent I have, and to pay attention to it and how I used it in my life. This didn't mean that I had to go out and form a band or create a CD, but rather, it showed me the importance of respecting it, identifying why it was a missing part of my life up to that point, and to begin to integrate it more fully into various aspects of my life.

"After that experience, I bought a full digital keyboard, and I have had a number of occasions to play publicly as well. Also, I've picked up playing the bodhran (an Irish frame drum), which I have been playing in a pub session band for the past couple of years. It's a lot easier to carry around, compared to a piano! As I think back on the experience I had with you, I've come to recognize, and value in a deeper way, the role of music and playing an instrument in my life. It is a key part of who I am!"

We can all take our passion—"a key part of who I am," as Leo Deveau described it—and turn it into our Calling. Indeed, living a life in which we avoid or deny our Calling is an unfortunate waste of the talents we've been given. Imagine your entire family, or organizations powered by people who have each found their Calling and who are using their finest gifts to serve the world—how extraordinary would your family or organization be? Or imagine if all of us were encouraged to invest in and pursue our strengths, so that our inherent or developed mastery became our Calling. Imagine entire teams and organizations comprised of bright, shining, inspiring people whose sparks had all clearly been discovered and ignited. When the spark is glowing, it is unstoppable. As Oprah Winfrey reminds us, "I believe there's a calling for all of us. I know that every human being has value and purpose. The real work of our lives is to become aware. And awakened. To answer the call."

A Passion for Pursuing a Powerful Calling

Scottish percussionist and composer Evelyn Glennie lost nearly all her hearing by age 12. Instead of becoming isolated from what and whom she loved—separateness—she has used her hearing loss to develop her Character and a unique connection to her music—oneness.

Evelyn Glennie was born in Methlick, Aberdeenshire, Scotland, and raised on a farm there. Her father was Herbert Arthur Glennie, an accordionist in a Scottish country-dance band, and the strong, indigenous musical traditions of northeast Scotland played an important role in young Evelyn's development. Other major influences were Glenn Gould, Jacqueline du Pré, and Trilok Gurtu. The first instruments she played were the mouth organ and the clarinet.

Her entry into the world of music was anything but smooth. After studying at the Ellon Academy, she applied for admission to the Royal Academy of Music but was turned down on the grounds that she could not possibly be a musician if she couldn't hear the music. They should have known better. The feisty Evelyn protested, asserting that she believed that young musicians should be selected for admission based solely on their ability to play music and not on whether they were missing some or all of their arms, legs, sight, or hearing. No lack of spark here. Somewhat taken aback by this feistiness, the Royal Academy ultimately accepted Evelyn Glennie, whose bold action forever changed the criteria by which not only young musicians, but all applicants, are selected for admission to schools, colleges, and training programs.

Evelyn Glennie excelled, becoming the first deaf person in musical history to successfully create and sustain a full-time career as a solo percussionist.

As the world's premier solo percussionist, she gives more than a hundred performances annually worldwide, spending over four

69

months in the United States, and performs with the greatest conductors, orchestras, and artists in the world. For the first ten years of her career, she was a pioneer in almost everything she did. In a live performance these days, she can use up to 60 instruments. She also plays the Great Highland Bagpipes and has her own registered tartan known as "The Rhythms of Evelyn Glennie." She has collaborated with, among others, Nana Vasconcelos, Kodo, Mark Knopfler, Bela Fleck, Bjork, Bobby McFerrin, Sting, Emanuel Ax, the King's Singers, the Mormon Tabernacle Choir, and Fred Frith. She has commissioned over 160 new works for solo percussion from many of the world's most eminent composers and has herself composed 53 concertos, 56 recital pieces, 18 concert pieces, and two works for percussion ensemble. She writes scores for film and television, having won two Grammys, and her first high-quality drama produced a score so original she was nominated for a British Academy of Film and Television Arts (BAFTA) award, the equivalent in the United Kingdom to the American Oscars. Evelyn Glennie was selected as one of the two laureates for the Polar Music Prize of 2015.

Glennie is considered to be profoundly deaf, meaning that she has some very limited hearing. She says that of the 100 or so articles that are written about her each year, the majority of them devote more ink to her hearing impairment than her performances. She believes that the media and the public misunderstand deafness, thinking that it simply means that a person cannot hear. Glennie's deafness, however, has not inhibited her ability to perform at the international level—her spark is too bright—she has simply taught herself to hear with parts of her body other than her ears. She regularly plays barefoot for both live performances and studio recordings, to better "feel" the music.

She explains, "Hearing is basically a specialized form of touch. Sound is simply vibrating air which the ear picks up and converts to electrical signals, which are then interpreted by the brain. The sense of hearing is not the only sense that can do this, touch can do this, too. If you are standing by the road and a large truck goes by, do you hear or feel the vibration? The answer is both. With very low frequency vibration, the ear starts becoming inefficient and the rest of the body's sense of touch starts to take over. For some reason, we tend to make a distinction between hearing a sound and feeling a vibration; in reality they are the same thing. It is interesting to note that in the Italian language this distinction does not exist. The verb 'sentire' means to hear and the same verb in the reflexive form, 'sentirsi,' means to feel. Deafness does not mean that you can't hear, only that there is something wrong with the ears. Even someone who is totally deaf can still hear/feel sounds."

71

Evelyn Glennie's life energy is invested in being able to 'teach the world to listen." One can understand the energy and the passion behind her mantra of *"making the difference"*—nothing means more to her—and this is her calling. She has chosen to model the behavior she is seeking in others by overcoming a perceived impairment and showing that, in reality, it is not an impairment. She is aware that she can influence the world most powerfully by being, as Gandhi put it, the change she wishes to see in the world. It comes from within her and emanates to others and inspires them. It is a spark that others recognize and find personally empowering. Her life is dedicated to bringing this message of awareness to people, inviting them to be more inclusive of those who are hearing-impaired, and demonstrating for all of us how to learn to listen better and with more awareness.

From Evelyn Glennie's example, we can see that a Calling is a way of using our gifts and talents to serve that comes from our center, from a place deep inside—our essential self—and it represents our essence—how we want to be more than anything else—because we believe in it passionately and because we want the world to be better through the expression of our gifts and abilities and passion—our presence and being. Obstacles—such as deafness in Evelyn Glennie's case—are simply issues to be worked with, utilized positively, or overcome for a person who listens closely, and acts on, the siren call of their calling.

What obstacles have you accepted as permanent blocks to living your true Calling? In developing clarity around your Calling, I invite you to listen to your heart, so that you can follow your passion and thus "hear" where it would guide you in choosing your work. This might lead to radical thinking, as it did for Evelyn Glennie—perhaps even ending your current work, if it feels like drudgery. At first blush, this might seem dangerous or foolhardy—but how dangerous is it to spend your precious life ignoring your talents, to stifle your passion and your gifts, and to be a wage-slave in a business or occupation that is uninspiring? This is the uninspiring experience of the majority of people. As Mary Oliver asked in her ravishing poem, *The Summer Day*, "Tell me, what is it you plan to do with your one wild and precious life?" Live the answer to this question every day. Life is too precious for a moment to be wasted or a gift to be squandered. Reflect on where your gifts and passion lie, and then pursue them. As Albert Schweitzer reminded us, "Success is not the key to happiness. Happiness is the key to success. If you love what you are doing, you will be successful." It is simply not possible to be inspiring while pursuing work that is uninspiring or deadens the essential self. You can't put out that which is not within. And it is a tragedy if we die with our music still inside us.

Passion Precedes Profit

You may have never heard of Sandra Boynton, although, if you have ever seen a "Hippo Birdie 2 Ewes" card, you know her work. This card has sold 10 million copies, and she has sold half a billion greetings cards altogether, along with tens of millions of books and CDs, which have garnered three gold records and one Grammy nomination. All this is not a job for Sandra Boynton—she doesn't do it for the money—she does it because she loves what she does, and of course, the result is that she makes a lot of money. It often works that way. Says Boynton, "I don't do things differently to be different; I do what works for me. To me, the commodity that we consistently overvalue is money, and what we undervalue is our precious and irreplaceable time. Though, of course, to the extent that money can save you time or make it easier to accomplish things, it's a wonderful thing."

The roots of this thinking may flow from what she describes as an "absurdly happy childhood" in Philadelphia. When she was two years old, Sandra Boynton's parents became Quakers and, as the third of four daughters, she attended Germantown Friends School. There, her father taught English and was Head of the Upper School, and, Boynton says, "the best English teacher I ever had." Boynton attributes much of her "upbeat offbeat" attitude to Germantown Friends' arts-centered curriculum, as well as its thorough integration of the values of pacifism, independent inquiry, and individualism. This independent spirit was demonstrated during her graduation ceremony at Yale (1974), where she received a *Special Master's Magna* somberly bestowed by Charles Davis, the Master of Calhoun, Boynton's residential college. The graduation audience was unaware that this honor was actually a fiction. Boynton's grade point average did not provide for any degree honor at all, but prior to the ceremony, she had convinced Professor Davis: "My parents are here, so I'd really

73

appreciate it if you could just mumble some Latin after my name."

Which comes first—the Calling or the money? The social self chooses the money; the essential self chooses the calling—so it depends which self is speaking. Sandra Boynton has built on her publishing successes by turning her prodigious talents to music, collaborating with Mike Ford, who lives five miles away in rural Connecticut, to produce children's albums. One day, when she was working on the album "Philadelphia Chickens," she mentioned to Mike Ford that Meryl Streep (a fellow Yale alumna and a friend) was the only person she could imagine doing complete justice to the song she had composed called "Nobody Understands Me."

The very next day, who should just "drop by her studio" but Meryl Streep? Not only did she agree to record the song, but she also suggested that actor Kevin Kline might want to record one, too. He sang "Busybusybusy." Among those who have since recorded with Sandra Boynton are Blues Traveler, Alison Krauss, Steve Lawrence and Eydie Gorme, Sha Na, Bobby Vee, Gerry & The Pacemakers, Laura Linney, "Weird Al" Yankovic duetting with Kate Winslet, Neil Sedaka, B.B. King, Patti LuPone, The Bacon Brothers with Mickey Hart, Eric Stoltz, Spin Doctors, Mark Lanegan, Hootie and the Blowfish, Natasha Richardson, Billy J. Kramer, and Davy Jones of The Monkees.

Clearly, for the essential self, passion and intention precede profit.

Here is what the passion that fuels a Calling sounds like, in Sandra Boynton's words: "I love what I do, I love the people I work with, I care very much about the value of the work I create, and I don't need more money than I have. This is not revolutionary philosophy. It's just common sense."

As my friend Marianne Williamson puts it, "Success means we go to sleep at night knowing that our talents and abilities were used in a way that served others."

The Passion of a Calling Trumps Obstacles

As we showed earlier, as one of the most eclectic and innovative musicians in the world, Evelyn Glennie is constantly redefining the goals and expectations of percussion and creating performances of such vitality that they almost constitute a new type of performance. One might expect her to have abandoned her dream of being a musician, given her profound deafness. But not only has she overcome this obstacle, she has used it to change the world—in much the same way that Helen Keller did. Glennie knows her gifts, though they may not have been obvious to others, and has honed them and used them to serve—the definition of a Calling.

As she crusades to "teach the world to listen," she explains: "If we can all feel low-frequency vibrations, why can't we feel higher vibrations? It is my belief that we can; it's just that as the frequency gets higher and our ears become more efficient, they drown out the more subtle sense of 'feeling' the vibrations. I spent a lot of time in my youth (with the help of my school percussion teacher Ron Forbes) refining my ability to detect vibrations. I would stand with my hands against the classroom wall while Ron played notes on the timpani (timpani produce a lot of vibrations). Eventually I managed to distinguish the rough pitch of notes by associating where on my body I felt the sound with the sense of perfect pitch I had before losing my hearing. The low sounds I feel mainly in my legs and feet and high sounds might be particular places on my face, neck and chest."

75

The reality is, when the passion and fire burn for a Calling—there is nothing that can stand in its way—not even deafness for a musician. Passion trumps obstacles.

What do you love so much that you would not call it work? As Mellody Hobson, President and co-CEO of Chicago-based Ariel Capital Management Inc., puts it, "I don't draw lines in the sand between work and life. When I'm working, I am living."

Turning Your Passion into Your Calling

Years ago, when I was the CEO of Manpower Ltd., I employed a salesman called Mike. He weighed 285 pounds, drank 6 pints of beer each day, and played 36 holes of golf for as many days of the week as he could—which was usually at least six. He was an awesome golfer. As his manager, I could not easily organize him, encourage him to follow any kind of structure, submit reports, or make sales calls. In fact, I couldn't put him into a box of any kind. Trying to do so, as I soon learned, was like putting socks on an octopus. But his personal production was extraordinary. Clients would call our office and ask to play a round of golf with Mike, so they could personally renew their contracts with us. Mike had a waiting list of clients wanting to get onto his dance card. Trying to remake Mike was not only pointless, but probably commercially unwise as well. I know a genius when I see one, so I supported him in every way I could and set aside my need for conformity and control. He was a fabulous and high-producing asset for our company. Mike's calling was golf—selling to customers was how he indulged his passion and wove it into his life—oneness, again.

I lead two lives. One is dedicated to teaching, coaching, writing, and mentoring. Thirty of Fortune's Most Admired Companies and 12 of Fortune's Best Companies to Work for in America are clients of my firm. And I speak to audiences all over the world each year. My other life consists of skiing in the winter and kayaking and mountain biking in the summer. I've skied for well over 60 years all over the world, with some of the best skiers on the planet, and I can handle most any kind of ski terrain. Although I have owned a ski home in the mountains for many years, I had spent too little time there because I had been constantly traveling on behalf of our clients— just like all the other non-Mike-like consultants.

One day, I wondered to myself, why can't I be more like Mike? I teach it—why can't I *live* it? How could I combine my two lives—my two passions really—into one seamless whole? What I have learned over the years from coaching others (as the Zen saying goes, we teach what we most need to learn) is that when I am following my Calling—my passion—and using my best gifts to serve, I become inspired and am therefore more effective and inspiring for others. Yet, far too often, we sigh and say, "Someday, I will do that."

So, some years ago, I decided to practice what I preach by initially offering two- to three-day retreats for leaders in my home 10,000 feet up in the mountains. These events are called the "Leadership Summit,"[21] and we teach leaders how to ski better, how to ski "double-black-diamond" runs in one day, and how to be more effective leaders. In addition to attending our Leadership Summits, some clients have chosen to bring their entire senior leadership teams to spend time with us in the mountains, and others have returned with their entire families. These private skiing and consultation events, and the Leadership Summit, are both opportunities to improve technical competence in skiing *and* develop stronger leadership skills—as well as strategizing and exchanging ideas or discussing challenges, and making new personal and professional friends.

---

21 See https://secretan.com/teaching/leadership-summit-in-co-ski/

Skiing is a great metaphor for all these. It combines elements of the social self—personal excellence, personal growth, physical exercise and conditioning, technical training; and elements of the essential self—the sense of oneness, the humility and awe one experiences in the mountains, friendship and interdependence with others, an honoring of the sacred, and a connection to the numinous and larger picture of life. By using the metaphor of skiing, participants leave the experience better skiers and re-energized and re-inspired leaders. Many experience personal transformations that change their lives forever.

In a typical winter, I ski over 100 days. People look at me when I mention this to them and they sigh wistfully, saying, "Oh! How I envy that!" But there are two realities here: 1) This is a choice—I have chosen this format and adapted my life and professional practice in order to embrace my two worlds and passions, and 2) It's not as blissful as it might sound—it's not all play. I rarely ski for an entire day, even though I ski most days during the ski season, but I also work every day, too, and many leaders will work very hard with me—to become more inspirational leaders through skiing. It's not a boondoggle—it is a big personal and organizational stretch—for my guests and for me. Marsha Sinetar wrote a book called *Do What You Love, the Money Will Follow*.[22] The advice is in the title. Life is too short to stifle our creativity—if we identify our passions and blend them into unique and valuable resources, we will develop magical and inspiring opportunities to serve and prosper. Funny thing, my dance card now looks a lot like Mike's!

---

22 Dell; Other Printing edition, 1989

Defining Our Calling

When Al Gore was running for president of the United States, he was following a path—perhaps one that met the needs of his social self. The pain of the Florida debacle marked the end of his 2000 election campaign, and he became only the fourth person in United States history to win the popular vote but lose a presidential election—in this case to George W. Bush. He retreated to his home and reflected. With encouragement from his wife, Tipper Gore, he began to build on his real passion—the decline of Earth's environment (his Terrathreat)—and to build a compelling message detailing what he calls "the most serious crisis we've ever faced." This passion eclipsed his earlier passion for politics, giving him, as *Time* magazine put it, "...freer rein to matters of the heart and spirit than he ever could as a candidate."

Says his wife, Tipper, "He's got access to every leader in every country, the business community, people of every political stripe. He can do this his way, all over the world, for as long as he wants. That's freedom. Why would anyone give that up?"

Said Al Gore, "There's no question I'm freed up. I don't want to suggest that it's impossible to be free and authentic within the political process, but it's obviously harder. Another person might be better at it than I was... And now it is easier for me to just let it fly."

Al Gore has trained thousands to broadcast his message; he has won an Oscar for his movie *An Inconvenient Truth* and received the Nobel Prize. According to Tipper, Al Gore is "now more comfortable with who he is, he is doing what he is most passionate about, that's why it's working."

It always works that way. Following our true Calling frees up our deepest gifts, thus creating the opportunity for us to serve at our best—and at the highest level and become inspired.

When we define our Calling, we are describing how we plan to use our (natural and acquired) gifts and talents to serve. If we first define and then use our gifts and talents to serve others and the world, we will live lives that are inspiring to us and to others, and we will align our lives with our Destiny and our Character.

Rob Ryder, former Vice President of Learning and Leadership Development at Centura Health, referred to earlier, describes his Calling this way: *To awaken souls to the beauty they can create, through my writing, teaching, speaking and musicianship.*

Rob's career involved being responsible for encouraging and supporting the personal growth of the leaders of a 14,000-employee organization. He and his team directed all training, learning, and curriculum development for all of the organization's leaders. He described how defining his Why-Be-Do® guided his work and life: "For me, putting my Character into words brought together my hopes and dreams with intentions and possibility. My Character Statement definitely describes the journey and not the destination. However, the Character Statement makes the possibility of multiple destinations clear. At the moment, I am called to live into my Character through my Callings of leadership, composing, directing, and performing music, and public speaking and presenting. As I learn and grow with time, my Calling(s) may change to reflect new skills, interests, and intellectual and physical pursuits. I believe, however, that my Callings will always be focused and guided by my Character, which defines the essence of who I am and will not change. My Destiny will be defined by the way I touch others and am touched by them as I live into my Character. One's Character exists in one's heart, whether it is memorialized in writing or not. Writing it down provides a concrete acknowledgment to oneself of the direction, possibility, and goodness within."

We can each be inspired by more than one Calling. Rob Ryder is inspired by leading and helping others to grow, directing and composing music, and presenting his ideas to audiences. I love to teach, to inspire individuals, teams and organizations, and to write. I am also a professional skier and an accredited ski instructor and a passionate kayaker and mountain biker. Like Rob Ryder, I blend all these different loves into one seamless life.

The great Persian poet Rumi wrote:

> There is one thing in this world that you must never forget to do. If you forget everything else and not this, there's nothing to worry about, but if you remember everything else, and forget this, then you will have done nothing in your life.

> It's as if a king has sent you to some country to do a task, and you perform a hundred other services, but not the one he sent you to do. So human beings come to this world to do particular work. That work is the purpose, and each is specific to the person. If you don't do it, it's as though a priceless Indian sword were used to slice rotten meat. It's a golden bowl being used to cook turnips, when one filing from the bowl could buy a hundred suitable pots. It's a knife of the finest tempering nailed into a wall to hang things on.

> You say, "But look, I'm using the dagger. It's not lying idle." Do you hear how ludicrous that sounds? For a penny, an iron nail could be bought to serve the purpose. You say, "But I spend my energies on lofty enterprises. I study jurisprudence and philosophy and logic and astronomy and medicine and all the rest." But consider why you do those things. They are all branches of yourself.

81

Remember the deep root of your being, the presence of your lord. Give your life to the one who already owns your breath and your moments. If you don't, you will be exactly like the man who takes a precious dagger and hammers it into his kitchen wall for a peg to hold his dipper gourd. You'll be wasting valuable keenness and foolishly ignoring your dignity and your purpose.

It's Never too Late to Define Your Calling

The first question then, is, "What do you truly love?" By this I mean, what is it that truly calls to you, that deep down, at a visceral level, you love to do, because you find it exhilarating and profoundly inspiring. What enchants you? What romances you? What creates magic in your life? What career path do you secretly wish you had chosen years ago? Do you see yourself as a "could-have/should-have-been" rock star, trial lawyer, jet pilot, neurosurgeon, forest ranger, or firefighter? What are your true gifts? Did you choose a career that met the needs of your social self but left your essential self unfulfilled—did you forsake your North Star? When you dream about a life that is the one that slipped by you—do you wistfully yearn for the clock to be turned back so that you could start over? If so, remember, as Al Gore has proven, it's never too late. Carl Jung observed, "Life really does begin at forty. Up until then, you are just doing research."

St. Francis, the son of a prosperous merchant, took part in several military operations as a mercenary soldier before he felt himself called to be a preacher and mystic at the late age of 27 (the average lifespan in the 13th Century was 31.3 years). In the last third of his life he founded two holy orders; he died when he was 45. Bill Wilson was 40 before he started the organization that would change the lives of millions—Alcoholics Anonymous. Rosa Parks was 42 when she signaled the beginning of the end of segregation and ushered in a new phase of the civil rights movement by refusing to give up her seat to a white passenger on a bus. Golda Meir became Prime Minister of Israel at 71. Grandma Moses *began* painting when she was 80, completed 1,500 paintings after that, and 25 percent of her paintings were completed after she was 100 years old! *It's never too late to rediscover your true Calling.*

Think of your true Calling as inhaling the memory of virtuosity not yet experienced.

The Optimum Potential Theory

Try this thought experiment. For argument's sake, let us assume there are a million different occupations in the world, from goat herder, mail carrier, law enforcement officer, university professor, physician, physicist, building superintendent, CEO, gymnast, schoolteacher, and tens of thousands more—you get the picture. And in any one of these there are endless numbers of specialties—there are hundreds of different types of physicians or researchers, for example—so perhaps there might be a million potential career options. Now let us imagine that there are an equivalent number of inherent gifts, talents, capabilities, skills, or know-hows, any one of which might be lying undiscovered within you or me. Could it be that genius is simply the perfect match between an individual's inherent gift or talent, and the perfect available matching opportunity? How else would you explain Albert Einstein, Mick Jagger, Thomas Edison, Alexander Graham Bell, George Washington, Nikola Tesla, Warren Buffett, John Lennon and Paul McCartney, Isaac Newton, Mahatma Gandhi, Eric Clapton, Leonardo Da Vinci, or Stephen Hawking? Surely, these geniuses were lucky enough to find the perfect match between their inherent natural gifts and the fortunate coincidence of exactly the right matching opportunity? How would I ever discover that I might have become the world's greatest concert pianist unless I could have evaluated every one of the million available options until I eventually found the perfect fit? For most of us, it would take many lifetimes, but geniuses are those who found a shortcut. For most of us, this option will never present itself because we may be listening to the wrong voice—the social self—when we would do better to listen to the essential self. As the examples cited in this reflection prove, listening to the social self will merely lead us to a "job," but listening to the essential self will lead us to a Calling. Which voice are you listening to? Can you hear the siren whisper of your Calling coming from your essential self? Are you open to listening carefully, and then taking the bold steps necessary to follow that path being suggested to you? If so, you will be taking another step on the journey towards greater inspiration.

I am reminded of the words of my late friend Debbie Ford: "Your mind can't take you where your heart longs to go." In the spaces below, write down those things that your heart is calling you to do and that you are gifted at doing—regardless of whether you do them now or not—those things that, if you had complete freedom, you would spend the rest of your life learning about and doing. Listen to your heart here, and try to ignore the editing voice that issues from your mind or your social self:

The true gifts (or skills) to which my heart is called are:

_____

_____

Perhaps you are inspired and enchanted by the path that you have already chosen and simply wish that it contained more ginger, more zing, more excitement, meaning, and fulfillment? You are one of the lucky ones if you are already in love with what you do. Even so, how would you add more inspiration, passion, love, and exhilaration to what you do now? How would you ignite your spark?

The work I do today needs more:

_____

_____

As you reflect on these thoughts, try to reveal within them the gifts that have been suppressed, overlooked, or forgotten. As Leo Buscaglia said, "Our talents are the gift that God gives to us... What we make of our talents is our gift back to God." Until our true talents and gifts are rediscovered, polished, and honed, and then offered in service to others, we will remain a shadow of our potential.

In his commencement address to Philadelphia's University of the Arts, bestselling author Neil Gaiman urged the budding painters, musicians, writers, and dreamers in the audience to think out of the box. He advised them:

> "And when things get tough, this is what you should do. Make
> good art. I'm serious. Husband runs off with the politician?
> Make good art. Leg crushed and then eaten by mutated boa
> constrictor? Make good art. IRS on your trail? Make good art.
> Cat exploded? Make good art. Someone on the Internet thinks
> what you're doing is stupid or evil or it's all been done before?

Make good art. Probably things will work out somehow and eventually time will take the sting away and that doesn't even matter. Do what only you can do best: Make good art.

Make it on the bad days. Make it on the good days too. And fifthly, while you're at it, make your art."

What are those secret longings for you? What is your "good art"? What, if you were to operate at your personal best, would you be doing with your precious life? What do you care about so much that you would *pay to do it*? If you won the lottery, what would you do? What livelihood would you pursue if you were being guided solely by your essential self, with no constraints being applied by the social self? What work draws perfectly on your talent and fuels your passion? What work rises out of a great need in the world, flowing from your essential self, that you feel drawn to meet? What lies at the intersection of your gifts, talents and passion, and the needs of the world? This is where you will find your Calling, your voice, the fullness of your North Star. This is where your Calling lies—the sweet spot where the gifts, talents, and passion intersect with what the world needs now.

Imagine working for someone who you know is passionate about inspiring you to do what you love, a leader who is living and leading from her essential self. This is how leaders become inspiring for those they lead and serve.[23]

The livelihood that would best serve my essential self is:

1. _____

2. _____

---

23 Please visit https://secretan.com/product/the-calling-meditation/ (CD) or https://secretan.com/product/the-calling-meditation-audio-download/ (Audio Download) if you would like to purchase a full audio version of Lance Secretan's Calling Meditation.

The next question for you to answer is this: "What path do I need to pursue in order to ensure that my talents and passion intersect with the needs of the world?"

_____

_____

Developing Your Own Personal Calling Statement

Here are some examples of Personal Calling Statements that may stir your creative juices:

Sister Nancy Hoffman (former VP of Mission, Centura Health).
My Calling is: *To mentor, partner and walk*
with others on their journey to wholeness.

Simone Gabbay (author and editor).
My Calling is:
To serve others through sacred writing and communication.

Ryan Hellman
(CEO and Founder of Hellman and Associates
[Workplace Safety Consultants]).
My Calling is: *Leading, inspiring, mentoring,*
and teaching health and safety professionals.

And my own:

To lead and serve others through writing, teaching, and speaking.

Putting Together Your Why-Be-Do®

By putting these three steps together—Destiny, Character, and Calling—we bring clarity to who we are. It affirms *Why* we are here, how we will *Be*, and what we will *Do* during our visit to this planet. So, we call these three combined statements our *Why-Be-Do*®—this is our North Star. By gaining this inner clarity, so rarely articulated by most people, we are able to move our lives forward with uncommon focus and passion. As a result, we re-inspire ourselves and renew our capacity for inspiring others. This is the first step in igniting our spark.[24]

Here is an example of a complete Why-Be-Do® from David Sherrod, leadership consultant and Higher Ground Leadership® Pathfinder:

Destiny (Why I am here): To help craft a more inclusive world.

88

Character (How I will BE and what I will stand for): To be an authentic and loving person.

Calling (What I will do): To model inclusivity in action through listening, learning, coaching, and teaching.

And now it is your turn:

What is your Calling Statement?

_____

First say to yourself what you would be;
and then do what you have to do.

Epictetus

---

24 To view the Why-Be-Do Statements of others and to post your own, please visit
https://secretan.com/tools/forums/why-be-do_forum/

Reflection Four:
BUILDING INSPIRING RELATIONSHIPS

Friendship is the hardest thing in the world to explain. It's not something you learn in school. But if you haven't learned the meaning of friendship, you really haven't learned anything.
—Muhammad Ali

Another way we ignite the spark within us is through relationships and understanding ourselves and each other better. Why we are here, how we want to be in our lives, and how we wish to serve—our Why-Be-Do®—these are the questions that have tantalized humans for eons. Becoming aware of, and embracing, our deepest, and well-considered sense of why we are here, how we will be during our time on Earth and how we have been called to serve, are the first steps.

We also become inspired by being connected to inspiring people, inspiring them, and, in turn, being inspired by them. It is hard to be uninspired when we keep the company of inspiring people—it is said that we are the average of the five people with whom we spend the most time.

The Use of Inspiring Language

There are many ways to build inspiring relationships with others. One way, on which we will focus here, is the use of inspiring language.

One of the toxic realities of our times is the violent language we use to communicate with each other. "My back is killing me!" we say, even though this is not actually true, but is actually a gross—and violent—exaggeration. Why do we use the language of war to make a point?

There is a word for a statement like this. It is called *hyperbole*, which the dictionary defines as,"exaggerated statements or claims not meant to be taken literally."

For those of us who do not feel secure enough in our own skin and fear that we will not be heard, or taken seriously, we tend to use words that we believe will gain greater attention. We do this in our emails and texts, too, when we use caps to make our point. A search on Google for "Chocolate cake to die for" generates 537 million references! Would you really die for chocolate cake?

We turn to violent language because we feel it will get the attention we deserve. But in doing so, we create collateral damage, because when we use the language of war, we unintentionally interfere with the well-being of those we seek to inspire or impress. Violent language is a blow to the essential self. Guns kill the physical body, but warrior language kills the spirit.

In my book *The Bellwether Effect*,[25] I share new research that shows how using warrior-speak, which is the go-to language of business, and increasingly, of society in general, makes people sick. If I say to you, "You kill me!" the pituitary gland sends a message that releases stress hormones into the bloodstream. These hormones arrive at the adrenal glands, which, in fear or anger, produce the hormone epinephrine. This triggers a quick boost of energy through the release of glucose, stimulating the heart, and increasing the blood circulation to the muscles and causing the adrenal glands to produce more than 30 different hormones. Medical researchers have noted that depressed patients are unable to maintain appropriate levels of T-cells (thymus-affected, helper and suppresser cells that fight viral, fungal, and bacterial infection), B-cells (helper cells that are manu-

90

---

25 *The Bellwether Effect: Stop Following. Start Leading.*
   www.secretan.com/thebellwethereffect

factured in the bone marrow) and NK-cells (natural-killer cells that spontaneously recognize and kill tumor- and virus-infected cells). This leaves the body more vulnerable to illness and therefore greater depression. This also suppresses your immune system and can lead to unnecessary worries and, because you are unprotected, to sickness. It is difficult to feel inspired when all these toxic biochemicals are coursing through your body.

The opposite is also true. If I say, "I love your dress," the word "love" will release a completely distinct set of biochemicals in your body, including oxytocin, known as the "love hormone." "I love your dress" inspires; "That's a killer dress" does the opposite. Which biochemicals are released by the brain depends on whether a person is experiencing pain and fear as a result of our communication, which releases stress hormones, activates the limbic system, and puts the body in "stress mode," or experiencing love and pleasure, which releases "uppers" that lower blood pressure, heart rate and oxygen consumption. Since the essential self and the body are one, our experiences of love or fear directly influence us to the core of our being.

The Biochemistry of Language

Albert Einstein once remarked that to describe love in biochemical terms deflates the magic of the experience. But we are being both literal and accurate when, after meeting someone, we say, "There was no chemistry between us," or "There was great chemistry when we met." Inspiration (love) and depression (fear) can both be explained in chemical terms. The science rests in the neurotransmitters, the chemical messengers of the brain, which play a major role in modulating our mood—whether we are inspired or depressed.

The neurotransmitter dopamine creates positive feelings associated with reward or a strong and positive connection (with people, animals, nature, physical items or activities), which lead to increased inspiration, causing us to be drawn to certain tasks and be more attracted to certain people. Conversely, reduced dopamine levels can contribute, in some cases, to depression, detachment, and a loss of inspiration.

Norepinephrine is both a neurotransmitter and a hormone, and together with adrenaline, it affects our "fight-or-flight response" and adds intensity to our emotions. It helps send messages from one nerve cell to the next. Low levels of norepinephrine, in some people, can lead to depression. There is a chicken and egg issue here, which scientists are still trying to understand: Does depression cause low levels of norepinephrine? Or do low levels of norepinephrine cause depression? What seems evident is that if we do or say something that depresses a person, it is likely to lower their levels of norepinephrine.

The neurotransmitter serotonin, often referred to as the "feel-good hormone," helps to regulate mood, and also affects the gut, sexual function, and blood clotting. Serotonin rises when we feel happy, and declines when we don't. And oxytocin, sometimes called "the love hormone" is raised when feelings of affection and love are present.

What we learn from all this is that we are unwitting manipulators of each other's biochemistry. How I engage with another person, including the choice of the language I use, can affect their mood (and our own). Therefore, the words we use are very important, and the relationships we choose, equally so. Inspiring people have a positive effect on our biochemistry. The activities we choose can change our biochemistry too—chores we intensely dislike will accelerate the flow of one class of neurotransmitters (unless we change out attitude towards them), and activities about which we are passionate, and love, will release different ones. We have formidable power, far greater than we realize, that can alter the well-being of others, and ourselves, by affecting the biochemistry, and therefore the moods, of ourselves and everyone with whom we connect.

Hardly anyone intentionally causes others to be sick, yet we sub-consciously do it every day. The language with which we choose to communicate creates well-being or sickness in others. When we communicate with others—even without words—we are effectively rearranging their biochemistry. As we see in the scenarios described above, inspiration or depression both manifest themselves as differ-ent sets of chemicals in our bodies. Most of this is subconscious—we can leave a meeting or a gathering with another person and wonder why we "don't feel so good." The answer is that chemicals that are toxic to our well-being not only alter our moods, but also our physi-ology. When we say, "I don't feel so good" after meeting someone, we mean it literally. How would you communicate with others if you knew that whatever you said, and however you interacted with them, would have the power to negatively, or positively, alter their physiology? Or their physical well-being? And, if their physiology became toxic, could they still be inspiring? If you knew that altering another person's physiology could cause them to become uninspired, and therefore, uninspiring to you, would you choose your words with greater care? How would you say, "I'd kill for that," or "love you to death," or "chocolate cake to die for," with different words, and in ways that would inspire the person to whom you are speaking?

Let's refer to Newton's Third Law of Dynamics again: If I use language that causes others to experience a rise in toxic biochem-istry, we are likely to experience a reciprocal, and negative, feeling. In other words, what we give is what we get. If we want to feel more inspired, we can positively alter the biochemistry in others, which will inspire them, and, in turn, cause them to inspire us.

93

Replacing Warrior-Speak
with Language that Inspires

Practice replacing the list of warrior language terms in the left column below with alternative and inspiring ways of expressing these popular, but violent, clichés:

Warrior Language	Inspiring Language
You're killing me	
Blow me away	
Blew it out of the water	
Motivated the hell out of me	
I'm dying	
If I told you I'd have to kill you	
You break me up	
Love you to death	
Plan of attack	
Dodge a bullet	
Bullet points	
If looks could kill	
Shoot me now	
Bulletproof	
Win the battle, but lose the war	
That's a hill I'm willing to die on	

Test these alternatives on a friend to see how they react. For example, say to a friend, "You are a pistol!" Pause and then say, "You are brilliant! I admire you enormously!" The sentiment is the same, but the choice of language is very different. Ask your friend to describe the difference they *feel*—in their body, not just their mind—after hearing these two different ways of expressing admiration. Do they experience any different sensations in their body? Is there a vibrational change in how they feel? Which choice of words do they prefer? You will be surprised at their reaction.

As Marcus Aurelius advised us long ago, "If it is not right, do not do it; if it is not true, do not say it." Let's be more aware and choose our words with care. To inspire others, we must understand the effect our words have on them. If your intent is to wound, use warrior language; if your intent is to inspire, use inspiring language. The language of war poisons; the language of love inspires.

95

Relationships are everything. When we love someone, it is wise to let them be the natural, perfect person they are and avoid trying to manipulate them into our opinion of "what is right" or how we think they *should* be. When we try to "change" people this way, we may simply be trying to see the reflection of ourselves in them. Building inspiring relationships depends on our being inspiring, not prescriptive. And it depends on the use of language that inspires—language free of violence and loaded with love. When we *love* the whole person—just as they are—and communicate with *loving* intent and with *loving* language, we create bonds that can last a lifetime. And that is inspiring.

Reflection Five:
THE ONE DREAM®

There is nothing like a dream to create the future.
—Victor Hugo

*If you don't have a dream, how are you
going to make a dream come true?*
—Oscar Hammerstein

We become inspired when we follow our dream. This is true in organizations, and it is true in our personal lives. In this Reflection, we will review two kinds of dreams—the dreams that inspire organizations and their employees, customers, and suppliers, and the dreams that individuals hold close to their hearts that inspire their lives.

A Corporation or a Movement?

Try this exercise with me for a moment: Take a piece of paper and draw two columns. One will be headed with the word "Corporation," and the other with the word "Movement." Now, in the first column, write down all the words that immediately come to your mind when you think of the idea of a "Corporation." When you have completed this, do the same in the second column: What words come to your mind when you think of the idea of a "Movement"—starting a new movement?

Corporation	Movement

Compare the two columns. Chances are that under the "Corporation" column, you wrote words like, profit, bureaucracy, hierarchy, controls, politics, lawsuits, budgets, meetings, fear, policies, marketing ploys, regulators, and so on. Under the column headed "Movement," you might have listed words like, passion, change, transformation, excitement, values, integrity, a cause, dreams, inspiration, progress, leadership, service, improvement, and so on.

Now ask yourself these questions: Which one am I trying to build? Which one inspires me? Which one do I we want to be?

Whether you work for a corporation or for yourself, either can be reframed as a *movement*. We can create institutions that stand for something, that will begin a revolution or a transformation, and that serve the world and make it a better place for us all. A movement inspires. A movement is birthed by a dream. It is a choice. What will it be for you?

Working with organizations globally, I have learned that the common, unifying experience among winning teams, great endeavors, and extraordinary achievements—is a dream. A dream lights our spark. Even more powerful is the fact that a dream can light the spark for an entire organization, as well as the communities it serves. A dream represents the uniqueness that can be found in groups of people who achieve the extraordinary—creating revolutions, overthrowing despots, founding religions or nations (or fusing them into one), climbing mountains, reinventing organizations, creating breakthroughs, building something extraordinary, inventing a new technology, or changing the way we live or think or how the world works. It is true of organizations, hospitals, sports teams, universities and schools, film crews, orchestras, states, cities, countries—even families.

Over the last 50 years of business theorizing and academic and professional development, we have succeeded in expanding our capacity to quantify, measure, and analyze, but we have stifled our capacity to dream. It has become conventional thinking that dreaming is too "out there" for a business environment. As a result, we shy away from talking about dreams in organizations. Instead, we have created "mission, vision, and values" statements. But the currency of mission, vision, and values statements has been devalued, their indiscriminate use and homogeneity rendering them feeble, uninspiring, and indistinguishable from everyone else's. While working with the CEOs of three of the largest healthcare organizations in America, I shuffled their mission statements and then sent them randomly to each of them. None realized that the one I had sent was not theirs. How can we *live* a mission statement if it is so boring, we can't even remember it or recognize our own from others? In fact, many organizations have reduced the process of developing a personal mission into a banal, multiple-choice exercise—three columns, choose one word from each. At one time, what was first intended as a spoof with the on-line Dilbert Mission Statement Generator, became an

Internet hit for unimaginative managers! The stale barrenness of mission, vision, or values statements pales in comparison to the inspiring power and passion that are embedded in a dream.

In organizations, we are in danger of making a reality of George Carlin's observation, "Some people see things that are and ask, Why? Some people dream of things that never were and ask, Why not? Some people have to go to work and don't have time for all that." Most organizations "don't have time for all that," and thus uninspiring mission statements are "rolled out" to be met by eye-rolling and feelings of déjà-vu. Simply put, great organizations have a dream, and the dream inspires everyone who is a part of it.

Identifying, Realizing, and Sustaining the ONEDream®

We call the process of creating a dream "The ONEDream® Process," and it consists of three phases:

1. *Identifying* the ONEDream®
2. *Realizing* the ONEDream®
3. *Sustaining* the ONEDream®

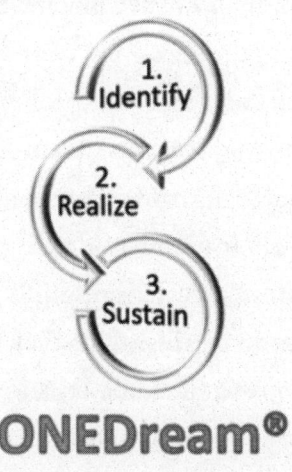

ONEDream®

99

I estimate that 10 percent of the energy and time is required to successfully complete Phase 1, 20 percent to complete Phase 2, and 70
percent to complete Phase 3. After the initial euphoria of charting
an inspiring new direction, and following the excitement of execu-
tion and implementation, sustaining a dream is by far the greatest
challenge.

A dream for an organization must be focused—which is why we
call it ONEDream®, not multiple dreams—just one dream that
galvanizes the passion and energy of the entire organization and all
who hear about it, are involved in it, or who manifest it.

What we are really discussing here is passion and how organizations ignite the necessary spark of excitement and energy in their colleagues, suppliers, and customers that will fuel the accomplishment
of something extraordinary—a dream. Not a five-percent increase
in market share or a ten-percent return on equity, or even being the
best in their field—but a bold, daring, impudent, audacious, outrageous, thrilling, exhilarating, and inspiring dream. This is another
aspect of how we ignite our spark—being a part of an organization
that is pursuing an audacious dream.

How did we land a man on the moon? The Russians had successfully launched Sputnik, effectively winning the space race, and
this caused Americans to be in a funk. John F. Kennedy's solution
was to define a dream, and it was a dream so powerful that thousands of people embraced it, made it their own, and thus made it
real. Indeed, it was such a powerful dream that it restored America's self-esteem, galvanized Americans, and inspired much of the
rest of the world. Dreams are like that; they transcend differences,
disagreements, and petty arguments, because the dream unifies us
at a higher level, engages us in a higher purpose, and fuses us—as

ONE. "Galvanize" is an important word here: while we may all have our opinions and even our disagreements, a dream occupies territory that is above these differences, and therefore it has a galvanizing effect on a group of people while leaving their differences intact. We may have differing opinions about *how* to do things, but we can be united on *what* to do. A dream achieves oneness at the highest level, *and* it *includes* the diversity of ideas and beliefs. And it is this elusive oneness—which, when achieved, is the highest form of inspiration—for which we are all yearning. Dreams are almost unique in their power to inspire through achieving oneness. A team that shares a dream is ONE.

We have worked with many organizations where the internal competition for resources, ideology, and the need for control or power have hampered the development of a unified vision. The creation of ONEDream® raises the aspirations of all concerned—inspiring them as ONE—because a dream elevates the conversation to Higher Ground, above the mundane and the pedestrian, to where the inspiration of shared ideals hold sway, leaving the squabbles over territory, power, and position to the lower ground.

Our historical heroes—Christ, Buddha, Lao-Tzu, Confucius, Mohammed, Nelson Mandela, Mother Teresa, and Martin Luther King, Jr., among them—all had a dream. In his famous speech delivered on the steps of the Lincoln Memorial in Washington, D.C., on August 28, 1963, Martin Luther King repeated "I have a dream..." eight times. It was his ability to articulate his dream that united thousands of people and inspired them to usher in a new era of civil rights and liberties. And that dream continues to inspire today.

Dreams are like that—they have the power within them to change the world. And great dreams, carefully executed, are achievable and sustainable.

We unlock the potential and power of organizations to inspire clients, organizations, communities, cities, and countries or the world, when we harness the megawattage of ONEDream®.

The Power of ONEDream® in Organizations

What would it take to change the world? We would need to pull the levers that could make the most effective change in the shortest period of time. So, which levers would we pull? In a previous era, we might have reached for the religious-community lever because the religious community was the most revered and respected of all human communities. This is no longer so. As the power, influence, and credibility (and therefore inspiration) of the religious community waned (according to the Pew Research Center, the number of religiously unaffiliated Americans has increased from 16 percent to nearly 30 percent in the last 8 years[26]), the political community assumed its role. But this eventually faded, too. Again, according to research by the Pew Research Center, "only two-in-ten Americans say they trust the government in Washington to do what is right 'just about always' (2%) or 'most of the time' (19%)," a precipitous decline from 1958 when 75 percent of Americans trusted government.[27] The result is that today the most powerful community in our society is business, which has become the most influential entity in the world. Indeed, if we wanted to change the world, the most effective way to do so would be to change the global impact of just four of the largest employers on Earth: Wal-Mart (2.2 million employees), Amazon (2 million employees), McDonald's (1.9 million employees), and Foxconn (1.3 million employees), all

102

26 https://www.pewresearch.org/religion/2019/10/17/in-u-s-decline-of-christianity-continues-at-rapid-pace/
27 https://www.pewresearch.org/politics/2022/06/06/public-trust-in-government-1958-2022/

of whom have millions of suppliers and customers. Each week, 265 million people shop at Wal-Mart alone. Nearly 5,000 items are sold on Amazon *every minute*. Within the orbit of just these four typical large organizations, hundreds of millions—perhaps billions—of lives are touched daily. If the leaders of these four organizations were to convene and commit to changing the world by honoring and inspiring their employees more, being more mindful of how they impact their communities and the environment, how they deal with ethics and leadership, how they pay their taxes, how they regard the spirit, how they enrich the human experience, how they nourish meaning and fulfillment—in short, how they lead, inspire, and enhance lives—defining their dream—they would change the world. And they could change the world faster than any other single grouping of people or organizations.

Yet many of us working in corporate jobs, or for ourselves as entrepreneurs, overlook this opportunity. Instead, many companies resort to tactics that may enhance short-term results at the expense of the common good—a triumph of the social self. This is uninspiring to employees, customers, suppliers, regulators, unions—just about everybody—the very opposite of what we are intending to achieve. The results are continuing messes and untidiness—of emotions and process. The "Great Resignation" during the Covid-19 pandemic was a long-time-coming reaction of employees to toxic work environments and represents just one indicator of the crisis of uncaring capitalism. According to a joint study by Great Place to Work® and Johns Hopkins University of 14,000 people in 37 countries, employees who are following a dream and experiencing meaning and fulfillment at work gain significant increases in well-being, and increased well-being results in those employees being three times more likely to stay with the company and three times more likely to recommend their employer to others.[28] In other words, they become inspired.

When leaders are invited to describe their richly imagined ONE-Dream® for an organization, remarkable things happen: they focus on aspirations that are not the usual corporate vanilla mission statements, and they describe their most extraordinary, outrageous, never-before-achieved hopes, often secretly held until then, because they now have permission to be fearless and imaginative, to think outside the box, and to be truly outrageous and unusually creative. Leaders come up with some remarkable ideas—hospitals who dream of eliminating all avoidable deaths, banks who dream of changing the world, corporations who dream of becoming environmentally friendly, regional communities who dream of becoming world-class centers of excellence and innovation, organizations who dream of a richly imagined future—and these are all from our direct client experiences.

ONE Dream for ATB Financial

ATB Financial (ATB) is a full-service financial institution headquartered in Edmonton, Alberta, Canada. It is the largest Alberta-based financial institution, with assets of $26.5 billion, more than 5,000 employees serving 670,000 Albertans in 244 communities through 164 branches and 133 agencies, a customer contact center, a network of Automated Banking Machines (ABMs) across Alberta, as well as Internet and telephone services. ATB was established in 1938 and has been owned by the provincial government since 1997. It has been named one of Canada's 50 Best Employers by *Report on Business Magazine*, one of the 75 Best Workplaces in Canada by the

Great Place to Work Institute, and one of Alberta's Top 40 Employers by *Mediacorp Canada Inc.*

With the arrival of a new CEO, Dave Mowat, the company decided to review its history, explore its horizons, and redefine its legacy. What Dave and his leadership team understood so well was that the image of banking wasn't always positive, and the methodologies of "mission, vision, and values" were tired and boring, and they recognized the need to refresh and inspire the company's morale and presence in the market.

We were invited to be advisors for ATB, and our research revealed by the strategic map (which we describe as the "permission space") we prepared showed that Albertans would support and encourage a financial institution that:

- has the ability to be customer-focused, to cut to the chase, and know what is important and necessary;
- is willing to take action—to be a catalyst that instigates growth and expansion, by
- providing brilliantly simple ideas and solutions that get to the heart of the matter.

This is an endless and self-reinforcing loop, which, if met by ATB's employees, would win the hearts and minds of customers.

From this, ATB reflected on their strengths and values—what was most important to them and how they could best serve their employees and customers in a distinctive way. Three key points emerged that spoke to their essence:

- Changing the world and making it a better place—being a significant, positive force in the lives of others

- Putting people first—not profits—in the belief that this priority, well executed, always accomplishes the profit objectives
- Helping farmers, businesspeople, entrepreneurs, families, young people, employees—everyone—to make their dreams come true

And so, the ONEDream® for ATB became:

"Changing Our World by Putting People First and Making Their Dreams Come True"

Realizing the ONEDream® means making sure that *everyone* lives the dream. In banking, the controls and hurdles for obtaining credit are significant, and it is often easier for a banker to say "no" than it is to work out a solution that meets the needs of a potential borrower. But saying "no" doesn't change the world, nor does it put people first or help this customer's dreams come true. In other words, saying "no" will not help ATB to achieve their ONEDream®. Clearly, the right answer for achieving these ONEDream® aspirations at ATB would be to say "yes"—but how is this best achieved?

Nolan Berg, ATB's former vice-president of Marketing, tells the story of a branch manager who was approached by a young man just two weeks after securing his first job. The young man had no credit rating, no references or previous employment, and he wanted to buy a used car. The manager said, "Given your background and lack of credit history, most bankers would tell you no." After describing ATB's ONEDream®, he explained that saying, No would not be *living* ATBs ONEDream®. He continued, "I am going to tell you yes. Here is what I want you to do: I am going to give you a credit card.

I want you to use it and pay off your account promptly each month when it is due. If you do this for six months, come back and see me, and I will lend you the money to buy your car."

Realizing the ONEDream® of ATB could not be achieved with a no; it needed a yes coming from a creative, compassionate heart.

These are not the kinds of creative and exciting aspirations or transformational changes in culture that fit easily under a monotonous heading of "mission, vision, and values." A much larger canvas is needed for painting magnificent ideas—organizations become inspired when they have a dream.

Everyone in the organization needs to believe in the dream, to trust that the dream is realizable and that when the energies of their entire organization are harnessed behind that dream, it will be achieved. An organization with 10,000 employees that harnesses the passion—the total energy of every employee, vendor, customer, union member, regulator, media, and others—behind that dream, begins a journey towards a previously unattained level of performance.

Many people have subjective views about what a corporate dream should look like, and it is unwise to make such momentous decisions based on "hunch," prejudice, bias, or majority vote—or even conventional research methodologies. Many leadership decisions—across sectors and issues—are made largely through intuition, or "gut instinct." They are, in the end, intelligently derived "best guesses." Leaders then often use tools, such as traditional market research, commissioned studies, and the opinions of those around them, to validate their best subjective guesses, even though these methods, as described earlier, have routinely been shown to be flawed. Sometimes this "research" is used to justify or "validate" personal biases or subjective opinions.

The creation of a corporate ONEDream® inspires employees, and their inspiration inspires customers and suppliers—and inspiration *always* leads to high performance.

Creating a Personal ONEDream®

Let's turn our attention now to the creation of a dream for you—your personal dream. *Your dream is today's answer to tomorrow's questions.*

Uninspired people rarely have a dream, or, if they do, they are uninspired because they have given up any hope of achieving it. As we reviewed earlier, we can live in the shadow or the light—the shadow can darken our path, or the path can be inspired and illuminated by the light, and we can learn from both. It is a choice, and it is up to each one of us to choose wisely. When we choose to identify, realize, and sustain our personal dream, we are choosing inspiration over defeat, despair, or resignation, and this choice invites the radiance of inspiration to shine into our lives.

We all have dreams, but, too often, we fail to realize them. It takes resolve, planning, and alignment—everything we do must, in some way, either contribute to the dream, or at the very least, not interfere with its attainment.

I have been a passionate outdoor athlete all my life. I don't compete, but I revel in activities that help me engage with nature. In Reflection Three, I described how we teach leaders to ski expert runs *and* how to live inspiring lives. My passion for skiing caused me to establish a home in the Rockies. It started when I suggested to my wife that we take a sabbatical and ski for six months. As we considered the ramifications of this on our lives, and especially my work, we raised the bar by creating a dream to own a place in a mountain resort in the American Rockies. My personal dream was,

"Living in Nature and Using It to Change the World." Eventually, we built a home in Colorado, and I was able to ski and continue my work from there for several months each year. In doing so, I wondered how to leverage this dream, and this led me to designing an experiential three-day event we call "The Leadership Summit"[29] I referred to earlier. Participants from around the world come to stay with me, and we teach them how to ski double black diamond runs in one day. (The double black diamond symbol ♦♦ represents the most challenging and steep hill terrain meant exclusively for expert skiers.[30]). We use the experiential part of the time to achieve two things: skiing proficiency, and a more inspirational way of living and leading—and we also view it as a metaphor for life.

This is how it works: First-time skiers fall into two categories. One group never ski again after their first skiing experience—estimates for this group range as high as 75%.

Those in the second group become passionate fans of the sport. Typically, they are introduced to the sport at an early age, and they learn very quickly—they are inspired. Some go on to race or even become professional skiers. The rest become recreational skiers.

Typically, recreational skiers continue to learn into their twenties, and then they embark on careers, get married, take on mortgages and financial responsibilities, have children, and have less time. Also, as they age, their bodies become a little creakier. Their skiing skills plateau, and their skiing becomes more conservative as they age. They become content with their existing skill levels, less interested in learning, and settle into modest aspirations for their skiing activities. As they move into middle age, they become less adventurous, and the caliber of their skiing declines. Eventually, they give up

---

29 https://secretan.com/teaching/leadership-summit-in-co-ski/
30 https://www.tevamountaingames.com/double-black-diamond/

skiing altogether. There are many exceptions to this trajectory, but it is a common pattern, and the chart of their skiing life follows the typical bell curve.

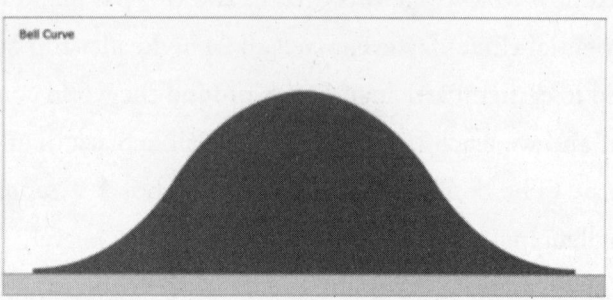

Skiing is a metaphor for life. As it is with skiing, so it is with many other aspects of our lives—how we are as skiers parallels how we are as leaders, friends, spouses, parents, and citizens—we start off with great passion and enthusiasm and intense learning, but this energy tapers off as our lives unfold.

When we bring leaders to the mountain and tell them that we can re-energize their passion for skiing, many express disbelief. But when they are on the snow and experience the inspiration that comes from a breakthrough, discovering that they can ski at levels they never dreamed they would achieve in their lives, they are converted. They become so re-energized and exhilarated that, metaphorically speaking, they feel they don't even need an airplane to fly home!

Then a higher-level conversation begins: Why do we need to go to the top of a mountain to make a breakthrough like this? Why can't we make breakthroughs like this in every other aspect of our lives? Why do we accept the myth that breakthroughs cannot be achieved quickly? Or that we can't change? Our curriculum covers Higher Ground Leadership® and skiing technique—both being merged seamlessly.

I am often asked, "What is the secret sauce? What is the technique you use to transform intermediate skiers into experts in one day?" The "secret" is getting people to let go of what they think they know—unlearning—a concept we reviewed earlier in Part One. The technique necessary to ski double-black diamonds is relatively straightforward—the really hard part is giving up the habits and techniques we have all become used to over many years. Pablo Picasso said, "Learn the rules like a pro, so you can break them like an artist." This is the secret.

No classroom, no seminar, no retreat, no MBA program, no theory, can match the visceral experience of making a physical breakthrough in one of the most beautiful, magical environments on the planet. Participants go home with memories and friendships that last a lifetime, a commitment to personal growth and change, and a new lease on life.

As you can see from this example, it is necessary to create the dream, then realize it, but even more importantly, to then sustain it. I have been leading these learning experiences (living my dream) for more than 20 years.

We are inspired by our dreams, especially if we are moving forward towards realizing them. The more progress we make, and the closer we get to our aspiration, the more inspired we become. What is your dream? What inspires you?

Nikos Kazantzakis said, "By believing passionately in something that does not yet exist, we create it. The nonexistent is whatever we have not sufficiently desired." And Walt Disney pointed out, "If you can dream it, you can do it. Always remember that this whole thing was started with a dream and a mouse." It starts with the thought—

an idea that has not yet been realized, that describes a condition that, when fully realized, will represent an ideal for you. The realization of the dream comes from passion and commitment.

And dreams do not need to be so "out there" that they are completely impractical. The late author and career/lifestyle coach Barbara Sher helped millions of people to create their personal dreams and then muster the energy to realize them. She taught her students, "Real dreams don't require you to abandon your family, quit your job, and move to Tahiti with your paintbrush. They just require that you search your soul for that deep dream you put aside and go for it. And watch your life light up."[31]

The power of a dream to inspire is palpable. If you consider what you really love doing, what makes your heart sing, and then pursue it with passion, your mind and heart will open, your life will change, and your adventure will begin. Sher added, "You must go after your wish. As soon as you start to pursue a dream, your life wakes up and everything has meaning."

Before we go any further, it is important to remind ourselves to ask the question, "To whom are you listening—the social self, or the essential self?" Reflect on this for a moment before we discuss how to identify your own personal dream. If we are listening to the social self, chasing "success" instead of joy, we may become disheartened because our dream will be about success, not joy. Inspiring dreams always focus on what brings joy—not just for ourselves, but for everyone. So, when creating your ONEDream®, invite your essential self to sit on your shoulder—imagine how you will feel when you realize your dream. Will it bring joy, or just success? Too many

---

31 *I Could Do Anything If I Only Knew What It Was: How to Discover What You Really Want and How to Get It*, Barbara Sher, Dell, 1995

successful people never experience joy. I am sure you don't want to be one of them.

And remember, it is never too late. C. S. Lewis said, "You are never too old to set another goal or to dream a new dream." It is never too late to become what you could have been, and what you still can be.

As you begin to identify and realize your own personal dream, keep your Why-Be-Do® handy. Dreams are like the North Star... it may take a while to reach it, but it will always be there, guiding you in the right direction, until you realize your personal dream. A personal dream is an important part of achieving, and living, your Why-Be-Do®.

The Whole Human®

We tend to separate our lives into "boxes"—the work box, the family box, the financial box, and so on. But nothing is really separate—everything is connected. Our lives are a holistic and integrated experience, each aspect touching and affecting every other aspect of our lives—professional, personal, intellectual, technical, emotional, physical, spiritual, and social. This is because separating these aspects of ourselves, and working on them independently, is based on the illusion that they are separate. For example, many people are searching for "work/life balance." But this is an illusion because when we balance something, it must be balanced with another thing, and in this case, we are proposing that two separate things must be balanced. But there are not two things—there is only one thing—it is called *life*. We are not looking for *balance*. We are looking for *integration*—the seamless oneness of our work with the rest of our lives. In reality, these "separate" aspects of our lives are ONE—if we touch any one of them, we touch them all. (See the illustration, The Whole Human®). I have been a coach for clients who wished to enhance one aspect of their lives without paying attention to the other aspects. But this cannot be done. If you wish to build a tool shed in your garden, you will need your health, some finances, some skills, permission, help, somewhere to put it, and support from your family. And if you only work on one of these aspects, the likelihood of success diminishes. If you dream of becoming a world-class coach, you will fail if you are unhealthy, if you have financial troubles, if you have a rocky marriage, if there is no element of service to the world contained in your dream, and so on. Every part of you must be fully involved, fine-tuned, and committed to your personal dream.

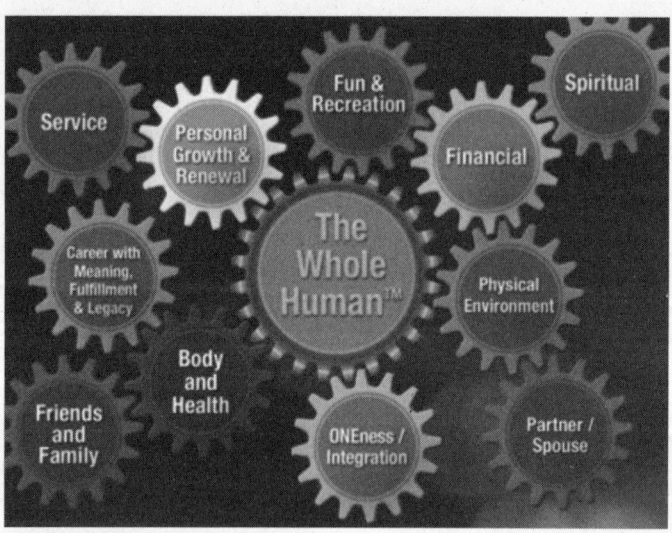

Some years ago, I was asked by a very successful entrepreneur to be his "leadership coach." He had built three companies and sold each of them for more than $100 million, and he was starting a new venture. We began our journey together, and after a few weeks, I asked to have a heart-to-heart conversation with him to discuss his future and how we would like to continue to work together. I explained to him that during the course of our conversations, I had learned three things from him about his life that it was important for us to work through together and with which I might be able to help: 1) He had not filed his tax returns for five years; 2) He was living in a relationship that had died, but he was avoiding the hard decision to end it; and 3) He had a drug-addicted son who regularly entered rehab, only to return to drug use again, fueled by the unconditional financial support my client provided—resulting in a co-dependency relationship and an endless loop. I told my client that we needed to discuss these things. I pointed out that these issues would affect his success and I wanted to help him resolve them. He said, "I don't want to go there. I hired you to be my leadership coach. These are not leadership subjects, and I don't want to discuss them with you. We do not need to discuss these other things!" I tried to explain that everything is connected. "If the IRS comes after you and throws you in jail, you will not be able to successfully build your business," I said. "If you come to work and try to inspire your team immediately after having an emotional argument with your common-law partner, your depleted energy and anger will be noticed, and you will be less effective with your team," I went on. "Your son's addiction gives you great pain and is affecting your decision-making and clarity of focus, which will not be good for you as the leader of your new business." He refused to accept the notion that everything is connected. So, we parted company—the only time I have ever chosen to end a coaching assignment in my fifty years of coaching. Everything is connected—there is no separateness—separateness is just an illusion, as we reviewed in Part One. Everything in our lives connects, in some way, with everything else.

Identifying Your Own Personal Dream

As you think about your personal dream, consider this list of the elements that make you who you are—The Whole Human®. Which ones need your attention if you are to realize your personal dream? (There is a free assessment tool here that you can use to measure each of these factors in your life: https://secretan.com/congruencewheel/).

1. Body and Health
2. Physical Environment
3. Financial Situation
4. Career with Meaning, Fulfillment, and Legacy
5. Partner/Spouse
6. Friends and Family
7. Fun and Recreation
8. Personal Growth and Renewal
9. Service
10. Spiritual Aspects
11. ONEness/Integration

What is your secret ambition—an outrageous idea that you would love to achieve, or perhaps an outrageous state of being to which you aspire? Consider one thing that you would simply *love* to do or accomplish, without considering any possible limitations (such as age, experience, skills, education, finances, health, domestic situations, etc.), and reflect on the questions listed below. What would be a secret ambition—an outrageous idea or state? Be unreasonable: George Bernard Shaw said, "The reasonable man adapts himself to the world: the unreasonable one persists in trying to adapt the world to himself. Therefore, all progress depends on the unreasonable man."

Give some thought to these questions:

- What is the greatest personal/professional achievement to which you aspire?
- What condition(s) would exist in order for you to feel profoundly joyful?
- What do you wish you had done, but never had the time for?
- What would you regret not doing, when your final time comes?
- What do you wish to be freed from?
- Is there pain or suffering in your life that you wish to resolve?
- What is the one thing you *must* do, or you will die trying?

And consider these three vital questions, too:

- What are you going to do with your life?
- What are you going to accomplish?
- What are you going to experience?

Next, remember to ask these three questions, because you can't do this on your own:

- Who are the individuals or groups upon whom you will need to depend for the successful achievement of your ONEDream®?
- What is the "permission space" they will give you?
- Who is the most important person in your life? And how will you enroll them as part of your dream together?

When putting a personal dream together, it can be helpful to gather a small group of confidants—friends, mentors, guides—and invite them to become your "Advisory Board," whose role is to offer advice,

REAWAKENING THE HUMAN SPIRIT

be your cheerleader, help you network, and support you with their own unique abilities and knowledge of you.

Here are some recent examples of personal dreams from my coaching practice:

- Client 1 (Chris T.): "To achieve financial freedom within five years" [3rd element: Financial dream]
- Client 2 (Rick G.): "To learn French with the Rosetta Stone language learning system" [8th element: Personal Growth and Renewal dream]
- Client 3 (Ryan S.): To leave the corporate world for a more contemplative and grounded life (he now owns the largest yoga school in San Diego, CA) [4th element: Career with Meaning and Fulfillment]

Sir Richard Branson, the entrepreneur and founder of the Virgin Group, which controls 400 companies, reminds us, "If your dreams don't scare you, they are too small." And George Lucas, the film director, producer, screenwriter, and entrepreneur best known for the *Star Wars* and *Indiana Jones* film franchises, puts it this way: "Dreams are extremely important. You can't do it unless you imagine it."

When you have chosen a question, and answered it, work on it and shape it into a statement that represents a personal dream—a statement that excites you, and which, if invested with the kind of effort described by Branson and Lucas, could guide and inspire your life today.

- Remember it is ONEDream®—not many dreams—just one that keeps you totally focused and inspired.
- Later, begin to define the steps you will need to take in order to achieve this dream. Break the personal dream into

a timetable consisting of manageable and incrementally ascending objectives.

- Use the Vector to identify your personal dream (see Part Four of this book and pages 84-93 of my book *The Bellwether Effect: Stop Following. Start Inspiring!*)
- What will your legacy be?
- Does your personal ONEDream® align perfectly with, and move you closer to your "Why-Be-Do®"?
- How will you live fully into the potential of your "Why-Be-Do®"?
- Does your ONEDream® speak to your essential self even more than to your social self?
- Twenty or fifty years from now, what will you wish you had accomplished or achieved, or had lived in your life?

119

What is your Personal ONEDream®?

_____

_____

One Last Thing

Now that you have identified and articulated your ONEDream®, write, on a piece of paper, the following:

- all the obstacles that stand in your way
- all the negative advice you have received
- all your self-limiting beliefs

When you are finished cataloguing all these constraints... take the paper, put it in a place where you can burn it safely, and SET FIRE TO IT!

···

If you want to build a ship, don't drum up people together to collect wood and don't assign them tasks and work, but rather teach them to long for the endless immensity of the sea.

Antoine de Saint-Exupéry

···

PART THREE

The Flame—

Inspiring Others

Part Three
The Flame: Inspiring Others

• • •

Once you have defined your North Star, the raison d'être of your life—your Destiny, Character, and Calling—your Why-Be-Do®; described it in brief words that inspire you and others; and grown into living it daily—*becoming* your Why-Be-Do®; learned to build stronger and more inspiring relationships, especially by removing warrior language from your communications, and identified your ONEDream®, you have achieved the first significant and necessary steps—the Spark—in the process of becoming, *and living as*, an inspired being.

As you will have discovered in our journey together so far, there is a sequence in this adventure of becoming inspired and being an inspiring person, and thus, reawakening your human spirit. As we have reviewed, we cannot be inspiring if we are not first inspired ourselves. We can do so for a while—we all have done that at various stages of our lives. But there are limits to how long we can sustain this, because we can't keep drawing inspiration from a well that is empty of inspiration. Having covered in Part One some of the ways in which you can fill up your well of inspiration—your Spark, we can now turn to the Flame—how we inspire others.

The spark ignites the flame—the fire within us, our passion and intensity, our informed and generous guidance with which we light the way—first for ourselves, so that we can then do so for others. Our flame illuminates and provides warmth. It is bright, always available, and nourishing. It is how others experience us and are therefore inspired by us.

The flame is powered by the way we live, and particularly by how we live out our values, because it is through the experience others have of us that they are served and grow, and the world, therefore, becomes a better place. People learn and develop, and we effect positive change in the world, because of *who we are*, more than because of what we know. When we coach, teach, lead, and engage with others, it is *who* we are that inspires, more than *what* we know. When I am teaching students to teach our work to others, I always ask them, "What are you teaching when you are not speaking?"

If the Dalai Lama walked into the room you and I are in, settled into a chair in the corner, sat there quietly for 15 minutes without saying anything, and then left, we would be inspired. Why? Because we know what he stands for, his higher purpose in this world, the values and beliefs that he exemplifies. We find his presence, his energy, inspiring. He is teaching when he is not speaking.

The values we live by are remembered by everyone we touch because they are what inspires them. As Maya Angelou famously put it, "I've learned that people will forget what you said, people will forget what you did, but people will never forget how you made them feel." We inspire others by being inspiring. We become the sun that nurtures the growth and bounty of others.

The Mother Teresa Theory

Some years ago, I was working with an agricultural chemical company. The company manufactured agricultural chemicals that farmers apply to their crops—fertilizer, pesticides, weed-control and nutrients. These chemicals are very sensitive to changing conditions and can be affected by many variables, such as too much, or not enough, rain or moisture; too much or too little heat; being applied too early or late; or too little or too much of the chemicals; and so on. They are usually applied in the early part of the spring growing season. If any of these variables should work against the farmer, the risk of a crop failure is significant, and if that should happen, the farmer can become very angry with the chemical supplier. Sometimes, they can become very aggressive, even abusive, when dealing with the sales personnel responsible for handling their account.

Over the years, the company had become used to this pattern of farmer behavior and so, each spring, they enrolled all their sales staff in a mandatory training course familiarly known as the "Dealing with Abusive Farmers" course. Upon hearing this as a newly arrived consultant, I reflected on this phenomenon for a while before offering a suggestion to the management. "Could we reframe this issue differently?" I asked. I proposed an imaginary scenario: "Let's invite Mother Teresa to join our sales team. We will give her a pair of big black boots and a Ford F-150 pickup truck. Her job will be to visit angry farmers. The phone rings. 'This one is for you, Mother Teresa.' Mother Teresa puts on her big rubber boots and hops into the F-150 pickup truck and drives towards the angry farmer's field. She parks the truck, steps out, and begins walking towards the angry farmer, who is striding aggressively towards her. As the distance between them closes, the farmer perceives that it is Mother Teresa who is coming into view and realizes that the company has sent her to discuss his problem with him." Then I asked the sales team a question: "When they meet, does the farmer scream abuse at Mother Teresa?" They all replied, "No." I asked, "Why? The farmer has the same problem, nothing has changed. What changed his behavior? The only thing that has changed is *who we are*. The farmer respects Mother Teresa so much that he would never be abusive toward her.

125

We change the behavior of others by changing our own. How can we model behavior that inspires the farmer to behave in a sacred and respectful way? How can we change ourselves so that *we are so inspiring*, we elicit a completely different response and relationship from him?" Who we are changes how others relate to us. It can change our relationships and provide the opportunity to change violent and ugly relationships into inspiring ones. When *we* change, we will see the change we seek in others and the world. In other words, the behavior of others is often a reaction to our own behavior. We don't change others' behavior by changing them; we change others' behavior by changing ourselves.

In the following six Reflections, you will be introduced to a set of values that you will be inspired to live by, and that will enable you to grow and flourish and become more inspiring for others. They are the principles that guide us as we make a difference in the world; they are what other people experience when we touch their lives and inspire them to greater things. We call these the *CASTLE®️ Principles*. Hundreds of thousands of people who have attended our Higher Ground Leadership®️ retreats, workshops, and seminars are living inspired lives today through the practice of the CASTLE®️ Principles. Many families use them as a "family code," and many organizations have adopted them as their corporate values, too. I hope you will find them equally valuable.

CASTLE®️ is an acronym that stands for Courage, Authenticity, Service, Truthfulness, Love, and Effectiveness. When fully lived, these principles are the path to becoming free from living small, un-inspiring lives, enabling us instead to live bright lives as a flame that lights the way for others, making a difference and lifting their spirits.[32]

---

32 Use the CASTLE®️ Survey to assess the degree to which you are living the CASTLE®️ Principles here: https://secretan.com/castle-survey/

These concepts are not new, nor did I "discover" them—they discovered me. We learned about these principles by conducting research to find out what people did *not* like about others, and our research revealed that people do not like:

- Cowards
- Phony people
- Selfish people
- Liars
- People who use fear
- Incompetent people.

Six easily identifiable types of people. From there, it was a short intellectual leap to surmise that living the opposites of these might be a recipe for inspiring others. After all, if these six traits are *uninspiring*, wouldn't it be logical to assume that the opposite would be *inspiring*? If the traits of negative and dispiriting relationships and lives, whether at home or at work, in politics, religion, academia, or our marriages, or among our families and friends, were described as these, then the simple solution might be to live their opposites. Validating this data across geographies, gender, age, and occupations showed that people were typically turned off by others who were not courageous, authentic, serving, truthful, loving, and effective. It made no difference whether they were CEOs, stay-at-home moms, front-line workers, artists or athletes—or whether they came from different countries and cultures. In fact, my colleagues and I have found that there is very little difference in what constitutes inspiration for people, regardless of their demographic or cultural origins.

There is nothing new to learn here, no great theory, breakthrough, or equation, because these are concepts that are as old as time, and they are within us already. At some stage in our lives, they were fully lived, typically in the earlier part of our life journey, but they may have become lost, and now we yearn to reclaim them. Consider the CASTLE® Principle of *Courage*, for example. When we had fewer stakes in the game of life, when we were youthful and strong, free of responsibilities, no mortgage or car payments, no bill-paying job to hold on to, we were naturally more courageous. Speaking our truth, and acting in accordance with it, was easy. As the years passed and we accumulated possessions and responsibilities, we inversely became more cynical, frightened, and drained of the power and passion from which our courage was drawn. Ironically, as we age, our courage grows again, because we become wiser (hopefully) and have less ambition and things to risk, so we can afford to increase our level of courage, which invariably leads to a happier life.

128

In the six Reflections that follow in Part Three, we will illuminate each CASTLE® Principle individually and consider how it could change who you are, and how you can conduct yourself as an inspiring person who lifts the hearts of others, and thus how you can help them to become more inspired and lead lives that also inspire others to make a difference in the world. Accomplishing this inspires us too—living the CASTLE® Principles and seeing their effect on others and our relationships is inspiring. And so, a virtuous cycle is created—the more we inspire others, the more inspired we ourselves will become.

Reflection Six:
THE CASTLE® PRINCIPLE OF COURAGE

Argue for your limitations, and sure enough, they are yours.
—Richard Bach

Merriam-Webster's Dictionary defines *courage* as "mental or moral strength to venture, persevere, and withstand danger, fear, or difficulty." Inspiring people embody mental, moral, and spiritual courage because we abhor cowards and love people with mettle—it's as simple

> **COURAGE**
> Reaching beyond the boundaries of our existing limitations, fears, and beliefs.

as that. And smart people do what works. My definition is shown above.

We use the word courage in reference to the bold actions of firefighters, law enforcement officers, and paramedics when they are at their best, or the actions of whistle-blowers who expose corporate corruption. In the first instance, a person's life is in danger due to the physical risks being taken; in the second case, people are risking their jobs by telling the truth—one is physically courageous, and the other is morally courageous.

In the lives of most of us, we are only infrequently required to display physical courage; but we are required to display moral courage almost daily. We cannot follow our North Star—our Why-Be-Do®—without courage, nor our ONEDream®. In fact, we can't really do anything new or different without courage. We can't say, "I am sorry" without courage. Or tell the truth. Or ask for forgiveness.

Or admit that we do not know, or that we need help. We can't say, "I love you" (especially in the workplace) without courage. We can't change our beliefs or update our thinking without courage. We cannot maintain an open mindset and embrace curiosity without courage. In fact, it will take courage to adopt the ideas you are reading in this book, and more courage to live them. And that is why courage is the first of the CASTLE® Principles. All these require courage. A lack of courage is a recipe for suffocating inspiration. "Courage is the ladder on which all the other virtues mount," said Clare Booth Luce. Think about the moments when you have felt most alive—you were practicing courage. And think about the moments after you failed to be courageous—in a meeting, or a conversation with a family member—did your lack of courage cause you to be disappointed in yourself? Did you wish you had been more courageous? Did you feel you let yourself, and perhaps others, down? Did this leave you feeling uninspired? Too few of us rise to the call of courage, but those who do are inspired and inspiring.

Conventional wisdom tells us that breakthroughs in life cannot be made without enormous effort sustained over a long period of time. In every field, there are many entrenched, traditional beliefs that present insurmountable hurdles to achieving the remarkable. This thinking is old-fashioned and unnecessary. *We should always be prepared to live the other side of safety—and this side of danger.*

Courage, Breakthroughs, and Skiing

Consider the art of skiing, for instance. For some, this sport is thought of as dangerous and frightening. As mentioned in Reflection Five (in the section titled Creating a Personal ONEDream®) when I am guiding and teaching people on the mountain,[33] I regularly enable skiers of intermediate ability to overcome their fears so that they can ski moguls (bumps) in their first half day and double-black diamond runs ("experts only" terrain) by the end of the first day. Many teachers will say this is impossible—but we have successfully taught hundreds of intermediate skiers to excel on advanced terrain in one day. We do this because it is a metaphor—as it goes on the mountain, so it goes everywhere else in our lives. The United States ski industry, for example, includes over 600 resorts, 32,000 professional ski and snowboard instructors, and 31,000 members of the National Ski Patrol. Although many excellent instructors (and I am an accredited ski instructor myself) help skiers and snowboarders to advance their skills, many lack the will, ability, or people skills to do so, and thus, those whom they teach rarely advance their skills in a meaningful way. Consequently, it is unusual to find rapid, radical breakthroughs in skiing or snowboarding ability, especially among those who have practiced snow sports for a long time and whose skills have plateaued.

131

Our lives follow this same pattern, with many excellent teachers, mentors, and coaches helping others to make meaningful change and grow, while many others are stuck in an unimaginative rut—consultants, academics, writers for learned journals, training executives, and coaches—still teaching old ideas in new times. As in skiing, leaders who have practiced their craft for many years and who have not developed and enhanced their skills find change and radical reinvention the most difficult. Even in our marriages and relationships, we can become stale, fail to grow, and invest in new

33 See https://secretan.com/teaching/leadership-summit-in-co-ski/ for more information on this

ideas in order to keep freshness and joy ever present. As a teacher of inspiration, I am part of a team that helps people and organizations achieve similarly radical breakthroughs by reawakening inspiration in their lives and organizations in a remarkably short period of time—just as we do in skiing. The secret to making a breakthrough in life or skiing is the same—courage (a belief in our own possibilities) and trust in ourselves and others.

Breaking through Limitations—"Unlearning"

It amazes me that so many skiers (and golfers, as well as other recreational sports enthusiasts) remain average or mediocre year after year, when they could do much better. I am equally amazed to see the same thing happen again and again in the lives of otherwise exceptional people. All this suggests that we are losing the strength of our courage muscles, because more than anything else, change requires courage.

In choosing how we live our lives, we exercise similar self-imposed limitations. Yet people regularly achieve breakthroughs in their experiences, in the meaning and fulfillment of their work, in the results they are able to inspire from others, in the love and joy in their families, in their service to communities and volunteer organizations, in their physical conditioning and health—and all of us have the power to do the same. As Buckminster Fuller said, we must "dare to be naïve," and naïveté can best be achieved through "unlearning"—but unlearning requires courage.[34]

We are able to teach intermediate skiers how to ski better and how to transform their lives in a fraction of the time that most people expect by igniting passion, willingness to learn and change, and a desire to improve—and most importantly, a firm belief that there

_132_

---

34 See "Unlearning Is a Precondition for Effectiveness" in Reflection Eleven.

are no limits. When we do this, we are the flame that burns brightly for others, inspiring and encouraging them, and coaching and guiding them to Higher Ground. We begin with courage, a word derived from the French word *cœur*—which means "heart."

Our Role as "Courage Coach," Mentor, and Guide

Recently, I took a group of skiers to the top of a 12,400-foot mountain. They were visiting with me in my mountain home to learn how to make breakthroughs in their skiing and leadership skills.

As we disembarked from the surface lift at the top of the mountain, a sudden snowstorm appeared, carrying big winds and causing visibility to decline to about eight feet. We were the only people at the top of the mountain, with no way down except on our skis. I huddled with my team in the storm.

"Here is the plan," I told them. "The only way off this peak is to ski down the side of the mountain into the valley below, for about 1,000 feet, as quickly as we can, in order to build up enough speed that will help us to accelerate up the other side. The route doesn't have many bumps or ruts, but it is quite steep. We won't be able to see anything, and you don't know the mountain. So, I will ski first because I know the terrain like the back of my hand." Laura Mc-Cafferty volunteered to follow me first. "If you agree, I would like you to ski right behind me as closely as possible," I told her. "Then everyone else can follow one after the other. Watch my skis—it will be the only thing you will be able to see in the whiteout. If you see the tails of my skis going up and down, you will know I've just gone over a bump, and you can brace yourself accordingly. If my skis turn, follow the direction they take. Trust me—we are going to be OK."

It went exactly as planned: a team of courageous, trusting, and safe skiers high-fived their success after we zoomed into the gloom together and arrived safely on the other side—all in one piece.

When we dare, it causes a moment of insecurity, but when we hold back, or try to play it safe, it causes us to waste our potential. Let's say it again, "We should always be prepared to live the other side of safety—and this side of danger." T. S. Eliot said, "Only those who will risk going too far can possibly find out how far one can go." Remember, your current safe boundaries were once unknown frontiers.

It is clear, then, that in teaching, coaching, mentoring, guiding, and leading others—and in living our lives as parents, lovers, children, and friends—there are some essential elements. When we play these roles, we must earn and build a trusting relationship with others. This trust creates a *loving*[35] space in which experimentation and challenge can occur, and in which we are able to let go of certainties—unlearning. This leads to change—and in change there is power. It takes little courage to cling to the stillness of the status quo—it is movement and change, which involves letting go of the familiar while embracing the new, that requires courage. Paradoxically, safety comes from the adventurous and the exciting, not the outdated systems of the past. In this way, we sacrifice what we are for what we can become—and that takes courage.

---

35 See Reflection Ten for a deeper discussion on the CASTLE Principle of "Love."

Playing to Win

....

COURAGE
Courage is armor
A blind man wears;
That calloused scar
Of outlived despairs;
Courage is Fear
That has said its prayers.

Karle Wilson Baker

....

Courage is fear that has said its prayers. Fear—the opposite of courage is how a large number of people—perhaps most—trudge through their lives, living, as Henry David Thoreau put it, "lives of quiet desperation." We are afraid of death and taxes, of rejection, failure, losing, judgment, disapproval, loneliness, looking foolish, being late, missing deadlines, illness, violence, alienation, losing our job, financial hardship, making speeches, flying, the dark, spiders and snakes and Hell—and the list goes on. So, we spend our lives defending ourselves against imagined risks. It is not inspiring to live a life in fear of so much that it shades everything else, and when we live this way, we are not inspiring for others either. If the predominant reaction to life is navigating safely through a myriad hazard, how do we become inspired or inspire others? When we live this way, we are *playing not to lose.*

But what if we *played to win*? (I define "winning" as "Going as far as you possibly can, using everything you've got.") What if we were able to embrace the opportunities in life instead of defending ourselves against threats? Most of the imagined threats—apart from death and taxes—are either avoidable or manageable. Fear fades when we play to win. When we live our lives embracing life, nature, love, friends, family, silence, well-being, fun, recreation, service, work, our Why-Be-Do®, our ONEDream®, spirit, and more, we are living large. Our enthusiasm inspires others; they inspire us; fear is forgotten, and we are even more inspired. We can't score goals if we stand inside our own goal defending it.

As Maya Angelou has put it, "One isn't necessarily born with courage, but one is born with potential. Without courage, we cannot practice any other virtue with consistency. We can't be kind, true, merciful, generous, or honest." And we cannot be inspired.

Think of all the things that make you anxious, that bring fear into your life. What is the worst that could happen? Share your fears (playing not to lose) with a friend and ask them for their opinion—they will probably dismiss most of your fears. But speak with your friend about all the things you love about your life (playing to win)—they will probably agree and even expand your list! Mark Twain shared this wisdom about fear and worry, "I have spent most of my life worrying about things that have never happened."

Courage is about being real, not heroic. It takes courage to do those things that people so admire in others: being vulnerable, admitting a mistake, apologizing, telling others that we love them, saying sorry, asking for help, listening, empathizing, abandoning a flawed decision, changing habits that no longer serve us, standing for integrity, and risking failure or criticism—these all require courage—and doing any of them inspires others.

Courage is a magical and essential ingredient for anyone wishing to be inspired and to inspire others.

As I mentioned earlier, the curious thing about the CASTLE® Principles is that they are within us already. There is nothing new for any of us to learn—we already own the capacity. We become inspiring when we recall any of the CASTLE® Principles that we have underutilized, bringing them strongly into our awareness, practicing them, and *living* them every day—starting with Courage. We were all courageous once—we have just forgotten how courageous we were, and we have settled into the easy road, the crypt of mediocrity. But we can get our courage back, because it was once within us. Let's reawaken and rekindle what we have lost—doing so will change lives—ours and everyone else's we touch.

....

All men should strive to learn before they die,
what they are running from, and to, and why.

James Thurber

....

Reflection Seven:
THE CASTLE® PRINCIPLE
OF AUTHENTICITY

If you call forth what is in you, it will save you.
If you do not call forth what is in you, it will destroy you.
—The Gospel of Saint Thomas

When we are authentic, we are living from our essential self; whenever we deny a truth, we are living from the social self—in other words, inauthentically. As Freya Madeline Starke phrased it, "There can be no happiness if the things we believe in are different from the things we do."

> ## AUTHENTICITY
> Being genuine, transparent, and aligned with our inner voice in all aspects of life.

And there we have the essence of authenticity—it is the capacity to be in alignment with the essential self.

Authenticity: Aligning the Head, the Mouth, the Heart, and the Feet

How many people do you know who say one thing, but do another? Or who think one thing and then say another? Or who feel one thing, but do another? Or who say but do different things all the time, causing you to think of them as unreliable or inconsistent? This inconsistency is uninspiring—to others, but also to ourselves, because we disappoint ourselves when we are phony, duplicitous, deceptive or inauthentic.

Authenticity is the alignment of head, mouth, heart, and feet—thinking, saying, feeling, and doing the same thing—consistently. This builds trust, and people *love* others whom they can trust. In other words, it is *oneness*—oneness of mind, mouth, heart, and feet—oneness (or alignment) of what we think, say, feel, and do. People love, and are inspired by, authentic people. What is important here is to understand that *the message and the messenger must be aligned*. Failure to do so sends loud signals of inauthenticity.

One of the most obvious examples of inauthenticity is the inability to admit mistakes—to own personal fallibility. Here is where the social self has a very loud voice—not the usual incessant and misleading whispering—but a yelling in our ear of the spurious message that if we accept responsibility for making a mistake, it will make us look incompetent, flawed, and lead to personal loss or hardship, or even reprisals and punishments. This is "playing not to lose," But admitting and owning our mistakes—and we all make them—is a sign of strength, not weakness, because it takes courage—the first CASTLE® Principle, and authenticity—the second one, to do so.

Corporate Authenticity

Look closely into any industry and you will find layers of authenticity and inauthenticity. The health-care industry provides just one startling example. Studies show that in the United States one of every 100 hospital patients suffers negligent treatment, some 250,000 people die each year from medical errors, between 7,000 and 9,000 people die each year from prescription drug errors, and 12 million Americans are misdiagnosed each year.[36] As alarming as these figures are—perhaps as many as 350,000 preventable deaths in health care each year—this may be an underestimate: studies also

---

36 https://mymedicalscore.com/medical-error-statistics/

show that as few as 30 percent of medical errors are revealed to patients. And a Rand Corporation study estimated that one-third or more of the more than $4 trillion spent on health-care treatments in America—more than $10,000 per person—could be of little value.

In health care, risk managers, malpractice lawyers, and insurers generally counsel health professionals, doctors, and hospitals to "deny and defend," warning clients that any admission of a mistake, or even an expression of regret, could lead to media and reputational fallout, loss of business, litigation, and endangered—even ruined— careers. So, the general practice has been to deny liability or culpability—an example of unrepentant inauthenticity—and this in an industry whose ruling precept is the Hippocratic Oath: *Primum non nocere* (First do no harm). And according to Dr. Lucian L. Leape, an authority on patient safety at Harvard, most doctors feel the same way. "We're pushing uphill on this. Most doctors don't really believe that if they're open and honest with patients, they won't be sued," he says.

Dr. Tapas K. Das Gupta is the chairman of surgical oncology at the University of Illinois Medical Center at Chicago and a highly regarded cancer surgeon. After viewing the X-ray that showed that he had opened up a patient and removed the wrong sliver of tissue, in this case a segment of the eighth rib instead of the ninth, he did an unusual thing: he acknowledged his error directly to the patient and told her he was deeply sorry. Having never made such a serious error in 40 years of practice, he told his patient and her husband, "After all these years, I cannot give you any excuse whatsoever. It is just one of those things that occurred. I have to some extent harmed you."

Though most health-care lawyers would wince at such an admission, the dramatic rise in malpractice costs and demands for action against medical errors have caused a handful of leading academic medical centers, including those at Harvard, Johns Hopkins, and Stanford universities, and the University of Michigan, to try a more authentic approach. The Veterans Health Administration, which pioneered the practice of open disclosure (authenticity) at its hospital in Lexington, Kentucky, in the late 1980s, now requires all adverse events, even those that are not obvious, to be disclosed.

Malpractice lawyers agree that what makes patients mad is not so much the errors as their concealment—the blatant deception and deliberate inauthenticity—and the injured party's concern that it might happen again. By quickly disclosing medical errors and offering genuine apologies, along with fair compensation, some healthcare leaders are attempting to reverse the loss of integrity perceived by the public, realizing that to do so will enable them to divert precious resources from costly and protracted lawsuits and channel them into learning from mistakes, while simultaneously diminishing the anger and frustration that so often feed a lawsuit.

141

Of course, the social selves of many attorneys will leap into the foreground upon hearing this news, prompting dark warnings that disclosure will result in a flood of lawsuits—but the opposite has proven to be true. Many hospitals are reporting decreases in their caseloads and savings in legal costs, and in some cases, malpractice premiums have declined.

At the University of Michigan Health System, one of the early leaders in authentic full disclosure, after implementing a fresh, authentic approach, claims and lawsuits over six years dropped from 262 to 83, according to Richard C. Boothman, then the medical center's Executive Director of Clinical Safety. "Improving patient safety and patient communication is more likely to cure the malpractice crisis than defensiveness and denial," he said, adding that since introducing a new approach, "the hospital's legal defense costs and the money it must set aside to pay claims have each been cut by two-thirds." The time taken to dispose of cases has been halved at the University of Michigan Health System. The approach became known as "the Michigan Model."

This change in philosophy engendered a new mood and relationship between trial lawyers and Mr. Boothman: the lawyers knew that Mr. Boothman would offer prompt and fair compensation for real negligence, but would stand firm in defending doctors when the hospital believed that appropriate care had been provided.

According to Southfield, Michigan, trial lawyer Norman D. Tucker, "The filing of a lawsuit at the University of Michigan is now the last option, whereas with other hospitals, it tends to be the first and only option. We might give cases a second look before filing because if it's not going to settle quickly, tighten up your cinch. It's probably going to be a long ride."

At the University of Illinois, greater authenticity produced the same results: the number of malpractice filings dropped by 50 percent in the first two years since the adoption of its program of authentic disclosure, according to Dr. Timothy B. McDonald, the hospital's chief safety and risk officer.

In one case, the hospital discovered an electrode that had dislodged from a baby's scalp during a Caesarian section. The mother, Maria Del Rosario Valdez, said that although she was unhappy about having a second operation to retrieve the wire, she appreciated that it was an accidental error. Her sister urged her to retain a lawyer, but she chose not to do so because she wished to avoid the angst of a lawsuit and believed that her injuries were not severe enough to justify pursuing a legal remedy.

Ms. Valdez said she was satisfied that the hospital quickly acknowledged its mistake, corrected it without charge, and introduced procedures for keeping better track of electrodes in the future. "They took the time to explain it and to tell me they were sorry," she said. "I felt good that they were taking care of what they had done."

These examples show how moving to higher ground, by adopting a practice of authenticity and living it, and weaving increased authenticity into our workplace cultures, creates inspiration—for employees (who experience an improved sense of spiritual integrity), for customers (who experience a greater sense of justice, compassion, and fairness), for suppliers (who experience a partner they can trust), for regulators (who realize they do not need to micromanage those people). These are the companies that employees are searching for because they are yearning for greater inspiration.

We love authenticity and despise duplicity and flimflam. Out of the 37 cases where the University of Illinois Medical Center acknowledged a preventable error and apologized, only one patient filed suit, and only six settlements exceeded the medical and related expenses associated with the cases.

In Dr. Das Gupta's case, the patient, a young nurse, retained a lawyer, but in the end chose not to sue, settling for a payment of $74,000 from the hospital. Said her lawyer, David J. Pritchard, "She told me that the doctor was completely candid, completely honest, and so frank that she and her husband—usually the husband wants to pound the guy—that all the anger was gone. His apology helped get the case settled for a lower amount of money." The patient received about $40,000 after paying medical and legal expenses and had the rib removed at another hospital, where she learned it was not cancerous. "You have no idea what a relief that was," Dr. Das Gupta said.

Straightforward, isn't it? The authenticity of a simple apology—the social self permitting—can cut costs, reduce anger, shorten legal proceedings, create learning opportunities, and bring the opposing parties to a place of conciliation. Transparency, openness, and authenticity are necessary conditions for getting to this place. Given the obvious evidence of these and so many other examples, it is a wonder that all of us do not yet appreciate what inspiring people have learned: authenticity raises the love others have for us, and this is inspiring. Corporate authenticity is simply the sum of the personal authenticity of those who work for those organizations. And as the examples from healthcare referred to above illustrate, even in difficult and challenging situations, people will be inspired by authenticity.

Personal Authenticity

Authenticity is a valuable practice across the entire spectrum of our lives. Whom would you rather know and rely on—a phony person, or an authentic one? Like so many of the concepts we are uncovering here, it becomes increasingly obvious which principles we should use in managing our lives if we want to be inspired—and inspiring for others. Oddly though, we sometimes find it easier to be authentic with others than we do with ourselves. And we often find it easier to discuss the authenticity—or the lack of it—in other individuals or organizations, than we do to *be* authentic ourselves.

And just as we find inauthentic organizations distasteful, we find inauthentic individuals equally so. And the reverse is true—we are inspired by authentic organizations, mainly because their cultures encourage and nourish authentic behavior, which enables them to attract employees and customers who value authenticity. We are inspired by authentic individuals in the same way. This is not surprising—we are all people—just in different settings.

Whistle-blowers are examples of courageous authenticity, and while most of us will not be called upon to demonstrate such extraordinary levels of authenticity, the role of the whistle-blower represents a powerful benchmark for individual genuineness and courage. If we are to be inspiring examples for others, then reciprocal authenticity is demanded first in our relationships with those inside our families, our circle of friends and work colleagues, and secondly, with those outside of those circles. Note the order here—we cannot expect to inspire others with our authenticity if we cannot even practice this principle with those in our immediate circle of family, acquaintances, and colleagues.

Authenticity: A Lesson We All Get—Eventually

Our social self wraps itself in the cloak of inauthenticity. But every one of us will eventually shed this veneer, even if, for some of us, it is not until our final moments on this mortal plane. Everyone eventually gets it—some sooner than others—but no one leaves without this lesson.

145

Eugene Desmond O'Kelly worked for three decades for the giant accounting firm KPMG International, ultimately rising to the position of chairman and chief executive. A graduate of Pennsylvania State University, with an MBA from Stanford University, Gene O'Kelly joined KPMG in San Francisco in 1972, became a partner in 1982, and was appointed to the management committee in 1998.

As he neared his fifty-third birthday, he was the epitome of the hard-charging American executive—guiding the direction of 20,000 employees, focusing on changing the culture, managing corporate strategy, paying $465 million to settle charges of criminal tax fraud, racking up endless frequent flyer miles, entertaining clients—and sacrificing home and family life. He was feeling, as he would later say, "vigorous, indefatigable, and damn near immortal."

The ground shifted beneath him one day, when he received the news that he had inoperable late-stage brain cancer. This news was accompanied by the realization that he would probably not make it through the summer. Suddenly, the wisdom kicked in: in his typical A-type behavior, he catalogued his colleagues, friends, and family into five concentric circles, with the inner circle representing those closest to him, and he realized that he had been, "a bit too consumed by the outermost circle. Perhaps I could have found the time, in the last decade, to have had a weekday lunch with my wife more often than…twice? I realized that being able to count a thousand people in that fifth circle was not something to be proud of. It was something to be wary of."

In the 100 days between diagnosis and his passing, Gene O'Kelly wrote a book (*Chasing Daylight: How My Forthcoming Death Transformed My Life*) in which he would allow that one should confront one's own mortality sooner rather than later. But the paradox of being so organized in his death was not lost on him. "While I do believe that the business mindset is, in important ways, useful at the end of life, it sounds pretty weird to try to be CEO of one's own death… Given the profoundness of dying, and how different its quality felt from the life I led, I had to undo at least as many business habits as I tried to maintain." And so, he commenced a journey of authenticity: he began to meditate in the mornings, to search for great moments, to transition into the next state, and reflect on his legacy for his two daughters. He met with his colleagues, friends, and family to "close" their relationships. And he came to realize that his thinking had been too narrow and his boundaries too strict.

"Had I known then what I know now," he said, "almost certainly I would have been more creative in figuring out a way to live a more balanced life, to spend more time with my family." His widow, Corinne, says this was his one regret. Although he had begun to find a better balance before he became sick, he ran out of time.

Authenticity is about being real, transparent, and balanced. It is about revealing our true selves with others instead of creating a façade with them. Authentic people are more committed to *being* than doing (the *Be* of the *Why-Be-Do*®)—to living openly in ways that inspire others. And most importantly, when we are authentic, we are honoring the essential self. We all learn this—in the end.

The Importance of Authenticity in an Inauthentic World

Have we lost our moral compass? Has the world become less authentic? Can we be authentic ourselves if we are the only ones living this way? If we perceive the world as generally inauthentic, can we be an outlier? These questions raise bigger ones: should we simply join the deterioration and become part of the problem? Would doing so be inspiring—to others, and ourselves? If we wish to see change, who is going to initiate it? If not us, then who? Doesn't this suggest that we should set the tone, model the behavior, and live the principles we wish to see in the world? And perhaps, by doing so, change it, and thus become more inspired ourselves from seeing the small but important changes our authenticity can effect?

We can rail against the world, but this solves nothing. Resolving to live differently, despite how the rest of the world functions, is a sure way to nourish our souls. Of course, we will often fail and be disappointed, and sometimes we will despair and be tempted to abandon our resolve, but what does abandoning our authenticity achieve? So, we really do not have a choice, do we? We need to be more authentic every day and inspire others to do the same, even if it is only a few people we touch, because it will all count in the end.

If we recalibrate our standards of personal authenticity, we will restore mutual trust in our relationships—the touchstone of inspiring people—so earnestly needed in the world. Of course, it is an enduring paradox that when we lead authentic lives, inspiration increases because we have taken the strong medicine it takes to *authentically* relate with others, while ethically bankrupt people engage in inauthentic, devious acts to conceal disappointing events, which leads to a steeper decline in inspiration.

We positively relate with and connect to others because of who we are—our authentic, essential selves—more than from what we know or the persona we create for others. We become inspired—and therefore inspiring to others—when we live from the principles we value most, rather than by the external forces of the social self. We are all yearning for greater authenticity, from politicians, leaders, corporations, health-care clinicians, our partners, children and friends—everyone. If these, and others, increased their capacity and practice of authenticity, we would change the world. And we would be more inspired.

In the words of Snoop Dog, "You got to be who you are when you are."

So, you see, this CASTLE® Principle of authenticity, like all the others, is already within you. There is nothing new for you to learn, just the need to shed the façade of your manufactured persona, to rekindle the authenticity, some of which, like all of us, you may have lost, and find it again, raise our awareness of it, practice it, and live it daily. Authentic people inspire others. As this happens, inspiration expands for all.

Reflection Eight:
THE CASTLE® PRINCIPLE OF SERVICE

I slept and dreamt that life was joy. I awoke and saw that life was service. I acted and behold, service was joy."
—Rabindranath Tagore

Every inspiring person whom you know, or who is your hero, or who is a historic icon—is, or was, a servant of others.

SERVICE
Willing, and actively supporting, the good of the other.

You will recall that the CASTLE® Principles were born out of their opposites, and the opposites of service are selfishness and self-absorption. We *love* people who serve, and we find selfish, self-absorbed, self-serving people *uninspiring*. One might think that this would be enough reason to orient our lives to serving others, but selfishness, greed, and personal ambition remain the modus operandi for so many. The world sustains itself through service, and when we serve (remember when we reviewed painting a friend's bedroom earlier?), we inspire. When we require that others meet our needs first, instead of first seeking to meet theirs, we are uninspiring and uninspired. Conversely, the gift of service to others is a gift to ourselves.

When faced with life-threatening situations, we often respond with the natural, primal, human default behavior—fear or attack—and typically, this is based on serving the social self. Even those of us who might hold Jesus Christ, Buddha, Mother Teresa, or Martin Luther King, Jr., as their personal heroes can still fail to recognize

that when we stray into self-serving, fear-based, or attacking responses, we are neither Christ-like nor Buddha-like, nor effective. At
the intellectual level, we understand that the response of a Buddha
or Christ, for example, would always be authentic love, compassion,
and service—under any circumstances. Even though we know this
to be true, the judgmental tune detectable in this message can sometimes grate and make it sound like pretentious sermonizing that is
naïvely disconnected from the reality of our day-to-day lives. After
all, we reason, if we were attacked by a mugger, for example, the
natural reaction would be based on safeguarding our own needs to
protect ourselves from attack. But, thankfully, not everybody takes
this position.

Not, for example, for Julio Diaz, a 31-year-old social worker from
New York, who had practiced the same evening routine for years—a
one-hour trip to his home in the Bronx on the subway, exiting one
stop early, which took him to his favorite diner for his end-of-day
meal.

One evening, Diaz disembarked from the No. 6 train onto a nearly deserted platform and headed for the stairs towards the exit. Suddenly, he found his way barred by a knife-wielding teenage boy.

Said Diaz, "He wants my money, so I just gave him my wallet and
told him, 'Here you go.'"

As the teen sought to merge into the shadows, Diaz called out to
him, "Hey, wait a minute. You forgot something. If you're going to
be robbing people for the rest of the night, you might as well take
my coat to keep you warm."

The look on the mugger's face registered, "Like, what's going on
here?" Diaz said later. "He asked me, 'Why are you doing this?'"

Diaz looked squarely at his young assailant: "If you're willing to
risk your freedom for a few dollars, then I guess you must really need

the money. I mean, all I wanted to do was get dinner, and if you really want to join me…hey, you're more than welcome."

Diaz instinctively chose authentic compassion—service—rather than aggression or fear: "You know, I just felt maybe he really needs help."

The two went to Diaz' favorite diner together and settled into two seats in a booth. Soon, Diaz recounted, "The manager comes by, the dishwashers come by, the waiters come by to say hi and the kid was like, 'You know everybody here. Do you own this place?'"

"No, I just eat here a lot," replied Diaz.

The boy's eyes widened in amazement: "But you're even nice to the dishwasher."

Diaz asked, "Well, haven't you been taught you should be nice to everybody?"

"Yea, but I didn't think people actually behaved that way," the teen replied, still not sure if he was witnessing reality.

When he asked the boy what he wanted out of life, Diaz said, "He just had almost a sad face." The teen didn't seem to have an answer.

When the server presented the bill, Diaz was faced with a dilemma—how was he going to pay? Diaz passed the problem to the teen, "Look, I guess you're going to have to pay for this bill 'cause you have my money, and I can't pay for this. So, if you give me my wallet back, I'll gladly treat you."

The boy "didn't even think about it," returning the wallet almost instinctively, Diaz said. "I gave him $20…I figured maybe it'll help him. I don't know."

Then Diaz used a cunning ploy; he asked the boy for something in return—his knife—"…and he gave it to me."

Diaz' mother later said, "You're the type of kid that if someone asked you for the time, you gave them your watch."

"I figure, you know, if you treat people right, you can only hope that they treat you right. It's as simple as it gets in this complicated world."

It's as simple as it gets in this complicated world.[37]

Simple wisdom, too: Serving others is a sure way to inspire them—and that's as simple as it gets in this complicated world. For most people who might be mugged, in all probability, their first reaction would not be to offer their coat to the mugger. But reflecting on this, perhaps it is time to rethink old ways, because service to others is more inspiring than vengeance or violence, as Julio Diaz has shown us.

Serving Is the Key to Inspiration

Sometimes we get depressed or disappointed, and therefore uninspired. It happens to us all. We have choices in those circumstances. We can choose to mope and feel sorry for ourselves. We can blame the world, people, the government, and anyone else who we feel, in that moment, deserves our venom. We can choose to numb the pain with drugs, sex, or alcohol. And then—where are we? Does this work? Do we feel better, or just anesthetized?

An alternative choice is to serve. When we are in a funk, feeling uninspired, the greatest medicine is to serve others. It takes our mind away from self-absorption, out of our pain, and into the gift we are sharing with another. When we see the smiles, experience the gratitude, and feel the joy of others, through our service, we become inspired. It is an amazing thing—serving others, meeting their needs, helping them to grow, or easing their pain, or hunger, is a gift to *our soul*—even more than theirs! Julio Diaz demonstrates this for us.

---

37 A short video about this incident can be found here: https://vimeo.com/178051564

Try this: feeling blue? Help someone. Serve them. See how you feel. Relish the gratitude you receive. Bring it into your heart. You will feel so much better—you will be moved from morose to inspired in the shortest time. And then do it again—it compounds. Everyone loves people who serve—so you will be loved, and that, you will find, is inspiring.

People First; Inspiration Follows

Of course, the question is, "Serve whom?" The answer? "Everyone," because we are all inspired the same way. But in the world of business, there should be a preferred ranking of "everyone."

Many people living in the West, and a growing number in other parts of the world, are staunch supporters of democratic capitalism. We have awakened to the need to sharpen the focus of our definition of capitalism by acknowledging that we mean *caring capitalism*— capitalism that embraces the interests of everyone, capitalism that will leave our world in a better condition than we found it—in other words, capitalism that serves. And this is the hallmark of the inspiring leader—the leader who understands that the world serves us best when we serve it first. And the leader whose Destiny is to serve others and help them to grow and make the world a better place than they found it—is a leader who honors the sacredness of others.

And this brings us to the perplexing issue of why so many people fail to understand that at the top of the list of people we need to inspire through service are those with whom we work—employees, associates, colleagues, and team members. If there is any priority ranking at all, then employees should top the list, followed by customers, then suppliers and shareholders—pretty much the opposite of what is generally practiced today.

153

A story is told about Southwest Airlines, who received a letter from a woman complaining about the absence of seat assignments, a first-class section, and meals. She also didn't like the boarding procedure, or the flight attendants' sporty uniforms, or the casual atmosphere. To top it off, she abhorred peanuts! Southwest answers every customer letter, but this one stumped them. So, the letter drifted through the hierarchy onto the desk of then-chairman Herb Kelleher for advice and inspiration. In sixty seconds, the legendary Herb had penned this response: "Dear Mrs. Crabapple, We'll miss you. Love, Herb." Southwest Airlines has been consistent in its commitment to its employees for decades. Said Colleen Barrett, Southwest's former president, "Our customer service package is totally dependent upon [our] employees. Without employees—and without the right employees—we would have, at best, poor customer service, and poor service means no more customers." The corporate aspiration that Southwest attempts to live up to each day is this: "Above all, employees will be provided the same concern, respect, and caring attitude within the organization that they are expected to share externally with every Southwest customer."

And there we have the key, exemplified by Southwest's priorities: employees first, then customers, then shareholders—completely upside down from the legacy airlines—and most other businesses. The airline business typically attempts to serve shareholders first, customers next, employees next, and vendors and suppliers last. Southwest Airline experienced 47 years of profitability prior to the Covid-19 pandemic, during which time nearly all the other major carriers, suffered significant losses, merged, went bankrupt, lost money, or went out of business.

In many ways, our misguided addiction to the external, the social self, at the personal level, is mirrored in our desire to do the

154

same thing at the corporate level. "Making the numbers," and all that this term implies, causes us to be intensely focused on how we will be judged, what the external world—the likes of Wall Street, shareholders, media, the Board Compensation Committee, Sarbanes-Oxley, academics who write case studies, competitors, and other opinion-shapers—will think of us. And often that means what they will think of *me*, the social self.

The shift to a greater awareness of oneness, towards the honoring of the essential self, leads us to serve *others*—the purpose of all of us. Because we are interconnected, none of us can survive for long through self-interest alone.

The most inspiring organizations in the world know that the routinely mouthed mantra, "The customer is our most important asset" is not sound. It's not that customers are not important assets (although the term "asset" is problematic too, since we don't own them)—the *employee* is the most important asset. If we serve and inspire employees well, they will serve customers well; but if we serve customers and overlook employees, or even if we serve customers better or *more* than employees, we will not retain an inspired team that inspires customers and realizes our ONEDream®.

Yet survey after survey shows that fear and intimidation, power, and aggressive behavior—sometimes passive aggressive behavior— amongst employees and their leaders are the norm in corporate life. My experience confirms this reality. Much of my work with leaders of major corporations seeks to inspire them to break their ingrained dysfunctional habits that sap passion, creativity, and inspiration, and seeks instead to grow the will to serve—first each other—the first team, as Patrick Lencioni calls it,[38] and then everyone else. We labor under the misunderstanding that it's OK to abuse each other

38 Lencioni, Patrick, *The Five Dysfunctions of a Team: A Leadership Fable*; Jossey-Bass, 2002

155

as long as we make the numbers. But as Colleen Barrett reminds us, dysfunctional employees generate a scarcity of customers. What's even more concerning is that *dysfunctional employees generate dysfunctional customers.*

It's true across all aspects of our lives. Just as the inspiring effect we have on others elicits a corresponding inspiring response, which positively accelerates, the dysfunctional behavior we project onto others generates a dysfunctional response, and this dynamic quickly accelerates into deteriorating—and uninspiring—relationships.

Many of us in our working environments approach marketing as a warrior practice. Warrior marketers pursue the conquest and domination of markets, crush the competition, develop "killer applications" and strategies, and disrupt markets with "category killers." The warrior mentality, epitomized for many by such books as Sun Tzu's *The Art of War* and Wess Roberts' *Leadership Secrets of Attila the Hun,* deploys tricks and cunning to extract as much from the customer's pocketbook as the law will permit—think about the indecipherable loan or credit card contract you have with your bank or wireless provider. Or the algorithms of social media platforms. All this manipulative behavior serves the social self and the attainment of short-term results—but it isn't inspiring. Inspiring work environments are those that invite collaboration with employees and customers through symbiosis, feedback, compassionate input, cooperation, and deep listening—and most important of all, empathy, *feeling* what other people *feel,* in order to develop relevant new products and services that inspire—all practices that recognize and rely on building inspiring relationships. This is mutual service— what Easterners might call *karma*—the awareness that what we give is what we get. The more we practice warrior behavior, the more it will be returned to us, and the more we serve—honoring the sacredness of the other—the more it will be returned to us, too. We have choices we can make—we can choose to operate from our social selves or our essential selves—at home or at work. Different results will occur, depending on those choices.

The principle of service—especially to each other—rests on the concept of oneness: the reality that we are all one and interconnected with everything. Failure to serve employees results in a decline in their energy, passion, positive attitude, and willingness to learn and to serve others—and eventually, leads to their disenchantment and departure. Customers sense this, and the level of service they experience declines as a result; this feeds back to employees, sapping their inspiration and deepening the negative cycle—it is all one. And when this happens, flames are extinguished.

Recently, I was sitting with a senior executive whose company had recently been acquired by a giant multinational. She was describing how a set of faceless managers had descended on her organization and delivered an ultimatum requiring her to terminate half her employees, many of whom she had worked with closely for many years. Throwing them away like discarded pawns on a chessboard, although meeting certain financial conditions of the acquisition agreement, recognized no faces, no hearts, no souls, no compassion, but met another criteria—"getting the job done." In these circumstances, the metrics and the numbers do get met because fear and intimidation prevail. But the effect is short-lived, because the people have not been served, and so the survivors dust off their résumés, update them, and scan alternative opportunities. The best, and most inspired, talent is the most in demand, so they usually leave first, and while others may hang around longer, even they may eventually depart, leaving the company stripped of the very asset that the acquirer should have valued most—its human spirits. While serving

157

the employees of an acquired organization may seem like an obvious need, in so many acquisitions, the acquiring company mistakenly believes that it is buying physical assets and brand equity, when it is really acquiring the talents, gifts, passion, dedication, and hearts of all the people who made the magic happen. Thinking we can keep the brand equity while eliminating the people who created it is the equivalent of banging one's head against the wall because it feels so good when you stop. Job one following an acquisition is serving the people who can realize the promise of the purchase.

Tolerate, Disrupt, or Quit

If we want to become more inspired, one wise step is to leave toxic, warrior-focused work environments that do not honor people or nourish the soul. If we find ourselves working in uninspiring or toxic workplaces, or for toxic people, we have choices: stick it out and be miserable—tolerate; be courageous and initiate change—disrupt; or be authentic and leave—quit. Many people can trace their lack of inspiration to a miserable work experience, abusive bosses, unsatisfying work and conditions and meaningless procedures and meetings—an environment where serving corporate interests comes before serving employees. Even if we quit for a lower-paying, but spiritually more nourishing work assignment, the hit to the social self will be more than offset by the boost to the essential self. If we become more inspired by taking this positive step, our enthusiasm, commitment, and joy will soon be recognized and, ultimately, bring material rewards as well. Too often, we fail to take this action because we are afraid (the opposite of courage) of the challenge to our paycheck, status, lifestyle and more (all social-self issues). But if we let our essential self speak, and we listen closely, we will realize that change and disruption is the only option. And when we are courageous enough to change, we are serving ourselves at last, and we begin the journey towards inspiration.

People come to work in order to be inspired by those leaders who serve *them* first, customers second, and shareholders third. Our relationship to our work, and the colleagues in that environment, is a key factor in our levels of inspiration. When we serve, we inspire.

Motivate (intimidate) or Inspire (serve)

On a recent trip I was booked on a flight from Pittsburgh. Before the plane could take off, a sudden severe storm appeared, causing the airport to be shut down. The chaotic situation that ensued was very familiar to any regular traveler. As everyone lined up to see if they could secure seats on flights when they resumed, patience was wearing thin, and tempers were flaring. A smartly dressed man was becoming increasingly frustrated and angry. It began to dawn on him that his yelling was not achieving the effect he was hoping for, and he realized that he was failing to bend the airline's scheduling to meet his needs. Utterly frustrated, and with a final burst of anger, he yelled at the customer service employee, "Do you know who I am?" The unflappable employee stepped out from behind her counter, and addressing the ever-growing crowd of frustrated customers, said, "Ladies and gentlemen, may I have your attention please? This gentleman does not seem to know who he is!" Her comment was greeted with laughter and applause by all except the smartly dressed man.

A few weeks later, I was faced with a similar situation, this time in Boston. I was booked on a nine o'clock flight, which was cancelled; the noon flight was full, and so the customer service employee arranged a seat for me on the three o'clock flight. I said to her, "This must be really difficult for you; it's chaotic here and this must be

159

very hard work for you. Is there anything I can do to make your day easier? I have plenty of time on my hands now, so can I get you a coffee or some water?" She looked at me as though I had come from another planet and then smiled. She gave me a quizzical look, and then she said, "Thank you! I really appreciate your offer, but I am fine. This sort of thing happens frequently; we are trained to handle it, and everything is under control." She paused for a moment and then said, "But you know what I can do for you? I could bump you to business class!" I said, "Thank you!"

In these two examples, we have a perfect case study. In any of life's situations, we have options: We can use fear, motivation, intimidation, threats, berating, and ranting, all of which, as one can see from this example, are rarely productive. Or we can serve and inspire. Why do we think that aggressive, fear-based behavior will bring about the ends we desire? How does this serve—let alone inspire—the other person? Even if we are sometimes successful when using these methods, the success will be temporary, only effective in the short term, and likely to fail in the long term. Short-term results quickly fade. Our short-term "success," if it happens at all, will come at a cost—we will reap subsequent resentment, separateness, and eventually, the same ugly behavior will be paid back to us—deflating any inspiration we might have previously enjoyed. People who live and behave this way are rarely inspired because such behavior comes from a social self on steroids, and this, in the long term, is profoundly unsatisfying.

But look what happens when we offer to serve. When we serve another, the offer—and the act—of service, inspires them, and our actions and the serving relationship we have built with them, moves them to inspire us in response.

We serve others by:

- listening more than speaking; listening to empathize more than to respond
- empathizing and accepting the whole person without judgment
- carefully listening to the *needs and desires* of the other person
- being aware and compassionate
- pacing ourselves, regenerating and avoiding burnout, so that we can be present with others
- being grateful for what we have, that others do not
- articulating a positive forward direction
- recognizing that we are *one*; another's pain is ours too, as is their joy
- engaging and listening to the essential self more than the social self
- giving the gift of service by being fully present and undistracted with another

And in serving, we need to ensure that we do not extend the intensity of our serving to where we sacrifice ourselves. There is a continuum between serving and sacrificing. The former inspires, but the latter does not, and instead, leads to burnout.[39]

Happiness can be achieved through acquisition, but this is always rooted in the present moment and can evaporate at any time, depending on what might happen in any specific moment. But meaningfulness is derived from, and is focused on, the future—our efforts to make a difference, how we serve. Service is the art of lifting

---

39 Take the free Burnout Survey here to find out if you are experiencing burnout: https://secretan.com/higher-ground-leadership-members/burnout-survey/

others, and when we lift others, we lift ourselves, and in so doing, inspire ourselves and others.

....

I don't know what your destiny will be,
but one thing I know: the only ones among you
who will be really happy are those who have
sought and found how to serve.

Albert Schweitzer

....

Reflection Nine:
THE CASTLE® PRINCIPLE
OF TRUTHFULNESS

Whatever satisfies the soul is truth.
—Walt Whitman

Why is truthfulness such an important and vital element of inspiring others? It is because we find the experience of interacting with a truthful person (as long as the truth is delivered with loving intent), to be inspiring. The emotional and

> **TRUTHFULNESS**
> Being honest and transparent in all thoughts, words, and actions.

spiritual impact of a lie or half-truth—the betrayal, dishonesty, and deception—is painful because it dishonors the sacredness of our relationships. The opposite is also true—it is not just the truth that we admire and that inspires us, but also the courage, authenticity, and love behind it, because truthfulness is fueled by these three. As Warren Wiersbe reminds us, "Truth without love is brutality, and love without truth is hypocrisy."

We are suffering from what I call "truth decay." A lack of truthfulness or truth-telling—or, to be more precise, lying—is one of the most damaging forms of incivility, and incivility has a corrosive effect on others, whether they are friends, family, colleagues, business partners, or those we lead. Incivility is the direct opposite of honoring the sacredness of others and a critical source of our lack of inspiration. As American suffragist Elizabeth Cady Stanton reminds us, "The moment we begin to fear the opinions of others and hesitate to tell the truth that is in us, and from motives of policy are silent when we should speak, the divine floods of light and life no longer flow into our souls."

The word truth is derived from the Indo-European root *deru*, which translates as "firm, steadfast, and solid," The word tree is derived from the same source because it, too, is "firm, steadfast and solid." Anglo-Saxons used the same word for truth and tree, and druids (the priests, magicians, and soothsayers of the ancient Celtic religion) derive their name from the same source: *dru* means tree and truth, and *wid* means to know; therefore, Druids were the tree-people who knew the truth.

Lying is an assault on the soul of another and is the mother of all incivilities. We have all known the value of truth-telling from an early age. The story (of uncertain origin) of George Washington is so often told, quoting his father, "Truth, George, is the loveliest quality of youth. I would ride fifty miles, my son, to see the little boy whose heart is so honest, and his lips so pure, that we may depend on every word he says." When, according to Washington's biographer, Mason Locke Weems, a six-year-old Washington accidentally damaged his father's beloved cherry tree with a new hatchet, the boy was compelled by his conscience to admit his misdemeanor: "I can't tell a lie, Pa; you know I can't tell a lie. I did cut it with my hatchet." Washington's father was then supposedly so proud of his son's rectitude, that he said, "Glad am I, George, that you killed my tree; for you have paid me for it a thousand-fold. Such an act of heroism in my son, is more worth than a thousand trees." True story, or not, this is the ideal we teach our children. What happened?

The Oxford Dictionary chooses a "Word of the Year" annually, and in 2016 they declared, "After much discussion, debate, and research, the Oxford Dictionaries Word of the Year 2016 is 'post-truth'—an adjective defined as 'relating to or denoting circumstances in which objective facts are less influential in shaping public opinion than appeals to emotion and personal belief.'" They continued, "The concept of post-truth has been in existence for the past decade, but Oxford Dictionaries has seen a spike in frequency this year in the context of the EU referendum in the United Kingdom and the presidential election in the United States. It has also become associated with a particular noun, in the phrase 'post-truth politics.'" What we learn from this is that the world may appear to become less inspiring every year as we devalue the currency of truth. It is easy to draw a straight line between cause and effect here: a decline in truth equals a decline in inspiration, whereas an increase in truthfulness equals an increase in inspiration. Lying is unproductive and uninspiring—everywhere. And this presents us with another straightforward opportunity to become more inspired and inspiring for others—being more truthful.

Finding Our Way Again

We are born truthful. Then many begin a journey where they lose the script.

A Junior Achievement/Deloitte Teen Ethics Survey found that 71 percent of teens feel fully prepared to make ethical decisions in the workplace, but nearly 40 percent of them believe that lying, cheating, plagiarizing, and violence are sometimes necessary to succeed in school, and half (49 percent) say that lying to parents or guardians is okay—with 61 percent admitting to having done so in the last year.

Less than half (49 percent) of these young respondents say that they look to their parents as role models, and many have no role models at all. Consequently perhaps, teens feel "more accountable" to themselves (86 percent) than they do to their parents or guardians (52 percent), their friends (41 percent), or society (33 percent).

Reflect on what this data tells us. They didn't make this stuff up—someone had to teach, coach, model, and lead them into believing they could accommodate the contradictions "Yes, I will make ethical decisions at work," and "Yes, I lie, cheat, and defraud at school." If our leaders teach children a moral relativism that accommodates deceit, corner-cutting, and spin, our children will bring this lack of moral clarity to their future roles in life, too.

Not only is it vital that we show others the incongruity of saying, "Yes, I'm an ethical person," and in the next breath saying, "Yes, I lie, cheat, and defraud," but we are each role models for others, and the behavior we model has the potential to encourage others. When we speak the truth, model it for others every day, with loving intent, the effect is to inspire others, even if we speak a truth they do not wish to hear. We can love hearing the truth sometimes even more than the message it contains, if it is delivered in an inspiring way. This bears emphasizing: always tell the truth; but always tell the truth in a way that lift the spirits of others instead of wounding them. The truth should never be used as a weapon.

Lying: The Result of Personal Cynicism

Lucy Kellaway, a former management columnist for the *Financial Times*, wrote, "I am a liar. This statement doesn't sound pretty, but it's the truth. So far today, I've congratulated someone on their new job, even though I think it a complete mystery how they ever got promoted. I e-mailed various readers thanking them for their interesting points, which I actually thought were tedious.

"If you work in an organization, I'd bet my shirt that you are a liar, too. We're all liars, but lies are necessary. The corporate world demands them. Indeed, it cannot function without them.

"There are loads of reasons for this. Workplaces are hierarchies. That means we kiss up and kick down. Offices are competitive, which means putting your best foot forward and selling yourself. Which usually means stretching the truth.

"The rules of office life also invite workers to cover up any infringements. So we lie about taking days off, being late for work, or slacking. Unrealistic targets and budgets also make lying essential. In fact, lying about the work itself is necessary to keep us doing it. Thus, we claim to be 'passionate' about what we do, when in fact we barely tolerate it."

This is a sad commentary for two reasons: first, it comes from a respected and influential source that sets standards of behavior and purports to provide cutting-edge thinking about business. Second, it is so cynical that it is deeply depressing, missing by a wide mark the inspiration and honoring of each other that most people so long for. Worse, it encourages the dishonoring behavior and lower standards we abhor. No wonder then, that "post-truth" has become a perceived reality and a new word in the dictionary. Lies are not only evil in themselves, but they cause an evil viral infection of the soul.

Research reported in the Journal of Basic and Applied Psychology described an experiment in which two strangers held a 10-minute conversation. The conversations were recorded, and several groups of two were included in the experiment. Each pair believed they were telling the truth during their 10-minute conversation, but after reviewing the recording, the researchers reported that 60 percent of all subjects lied within 10 minutes, and on average, the participants lied 2.92 times in that time.

As you will have discovered by now, the CASTLE® Principles are interconnected and interdependent. It takes courage to tell the truth; it also requires us to be authentic; and it is an act of service to another person. *When we lie, we are serving ourselves; when we tell the truth, we are serving another.* In a "post-truth" society, where everyone expects a lack of truthfulness, being truthful is a distinctive behavior that others notice and admire. In other words, if we have become numb to the sea of lies in our media, politics, workplaces, marketing and labeling, resumes, dating websites, and so on, then truthfulness shows up as a refreshing and welcome difference. It is inspiring. Being distinctive in this way is not only inspiring for the truthteller, because we feel true to our essential selves, but it is also inspiring to the person hearing the truth.

The Guidelines for Truthfulness

168

As stated earlier, the truth is not a weapon. As the late Canadian humor columnist for *The Globe and Mail*, Richard J. Needham, reminds us, "People who are brutally honest get more satisfaction out of the brutality than out of the honesty." This should never be our intention. So here are some guidelines for truth-telling:

1. **Safety:** We make it safe to tell the truth. There will be no recriminations against, or punishment of, truth-tellers. We are human; if we are punished for telling the truth, we will not do so again.

2. **Inspiration:** The truth is not a weapon. We will endeavor never to wound with the truth. We tell the truth in a helpful and positive way. When we tell the truth, we will do so in a way that is inspiring for the other person.

3. **Taking the necessary time:** We do not avoid telling the truth because we are too lazy, or too busy, to think through

how we would say it in a way that inspires. Although it takes more effort to be truthful than it does to lie, we will avoid taking this easy route. We renounce this laziness and invest the time and energy to be truthful in a helpful and inspiring way.

4. **Starting Now:** This is the beginning of our mutual truth-telling. What has gone before is irrelevant. You may think that my past behavior does not qualify me to now become a truthteller, but my past is irrelevant if I have decided to turn over a new leaf and be more truthful going forward. Please judge me on the future, not the past.

A Truth-Telling Exercise

Try this experiment to evaluate your truthfulness. Listed below are 5 questions. Please answer them quickly, without too much analysis, using a number on the following scale: 0 is NO and 10 is YES. *Complete your answers before reading further.* Put your answer to the question, using the numbers from this scale, in the right-hand box:

1. I always tell the truth	
2. I have never taken anything that was not mine	
3. I am never intimidated	
4. I am always the best at whatever I do	
5. I like everyone whom I know	
TOTAL	

Total up your numbered answers—your total will probably be between 0 and 50.

Now let's analyze your responses. If you have any number higher than zero, you are probably playing fast and loose with the truth! Why? Take a look at the instructions again. The scale you were offered only had two numbers—0 is NO and 10 is YES—not a range on a scale from 0 to 10. Secondly, if you answered "7," for example, to the question, "I *always* tell the truth," this is an impossibility. None of us can *always* do something seven out of ten times! The only possible answer to each of these questions is zero.

I do not conduct this little experiment to trick you; I do so to point out how sloppy we have become when it comes to truthfulness. None of us will *always* tell the truth—I doubt that even the greatest sages and saints *always* told the truth. But we all have the option to improve our truthfulness—to avoid, as in the data referred to earlier—lying, even unintentionally, nearly three times every ten minutes. We can do better. And, if we try to do so, we will immediately be more inspiring, and more inspired ourselves. As George Orwell said, "In a time of universal deceit-telling the truth is a revolutionary act." The freedom we experience when we tell the truth will inspire us.

Telling the Truth in an Inspiring Way

Some years ago, I was consulting with a major organization, and my first meeting with them was in a conference room attended by their 32 CEOs. I began sharing some of the ideas I am sharing with you in this book, and one of the CEOs, Tom Anderson, stood up and railed into me with a withering personal attack. He said, "Lance, you don't understand this company. Your ideas are flaky—you must be from California! This 'touchy-feely' stuff will never work here. It is way too 'fluffy' for us, and our employees will laugh at us if we suggest these goofy ideas. You are disconnected from reality, and we should all go home now—and so should you!" Then Tom sat down. The air was electric, everyone was holding their breath, wondering what was going to happen next. So was I! I thought to myself, "Breathe! Don't say anything stupid. I am either about to lose a client on my first day with them, or I am about to make a breakthrough." I took a deep breath, paused, and then I said to Tom, "I think I know what you are trying to say to me, Tom, but could I ask you, please, to say it again, in a way that is inspiring?"

Everyone was still holding their breath. Tom got up and said, "Yes, I can do that," and he delivered a reasoned, and intelligent, non-emotional, insult-free, rationale describing why he was concerned and afraid that this much transformational and radical change being introduced so quickly in the organization could be counterproductive. Everyone in the room began to breathe again. I spent many years helping this company becoming one of the best in its industry, and Tom and I became the best of friends.

Being an inspiring truthteller does not mean we have to hide the truth, or our deeply held beliefs, or manipulate it to please the listener. It means we need to deliver the truth, with courage, authenticity, and compassion, asking ourselves, "Will my truth, which I am about to share with this person, inspire them?" When we tell the truth we must strive to help the other person feel larger, not smaller, while not compromising our own values—being true to our essential selves.

Often when we are faced with a challenge—a decision point— our natural reaction is to hunker down and hope that bombast and denial will tide us over until the challenge passes. This is the exact moment when people most earnestly look to us for cues about the strength of our integrity. As we speak our truth, we must ask these questions: Will my social self or my essential self determine the actions I will take? Will I be true to my North Star? Will I be modelling my Character Statement? Will my Why-Be-Do® guide my next steps? Will the action, plan, or decision be inspiring? Will what I am about to say serve my Destiny? Will I be a person that inspires with my truthfulness?

Lying by Whitewashing the Truth

Often, we hear dishonest jargon and euphemisms, designed to "spin" the truth, and this is one of the subtlest and most insidious forms of lying. "Shrinkflation" is a subtle form of lying, because it is an attempt to confuse and mislead customers by hiding the fact that the price of a product has remained the same while the size has declined.

When a major telecommunications company laid off 9,000 employees, they issued a press release describing the action as a "synergy-related headcount adjustment goal." Deceptive bafflegab like this demoralizes people and undermines the credibility of the business because it violates *all* of the CASTLE® Principles, including Truthfulness. Uninspiring businesses accept and condone this form of weasel-worded language as standard practice in the mistaken belief that it makes the action appear to be more noble: a technology company recently described the discarding of 1,600 employees as "actions to simplify our organization," and other firms resort to slippery pseudo-truths such as, "reduction in force (RIF)," "offboarding," "rationalizing," "surplussing," "de-verticalization," "strategic review of strategies," "rebalancing the workforce," and "restructuring." As Alfred North Whitehead reminded us, "There are no whole truths: all truths are half-truths. It is trying to treat them as whole truths that plays the devil."

I have noticed that entrepreneurs and businesses who commit to becoming a band of truth-tellers experience a sharp increase in morale, employee and customer satisfaction, performance, and inspiration. The commitment to kick it up a notch—to Higher Ground Leadership®—by rededicating ourselves to truth-telling, boosts self-esteem and is deeply inspiring because it raises our pride in our colleagues. We know we stand for something that is above average and noble. Because the demand for truth always exceeds the supply, a commitment to truthfulness is a simple approach to moving the inspiration needle in workplaces and in our personal lives, and a sure way for each of us to return to the script. After all, it is not a context-sensitive subject—we can't live as truthtellers at home and liars at work, and if we did, it would drive us—and everyone else—crazy! As Albert Schweitzer said, "Truth has no special time of its own. Its hour is now—always." We *love* and admire people who tell the truth, because we respect their authenticity, morality, and desire to honor the sacredness of others—and few fail to be inspired by such behavior.

173

In all aspects of our lives, the greatest homage we can pay to truth is to use it. Mahatma Gandhi often quoted the Sanskrit proverb, "There is no religion higher than truth." He also said, "Truth is one; paths are many."

Our friends, family, and work colleagues quite rightly expect us to model the standards we expect from them. We may exhort each other to speak the truth, but if we "spin" the truth, we have no right to expect anything better than the shabby standards we have ourselves established. When we raise the bar, setting a higher standard of truthfulness, we introduce a new level of excitement and inspiration, because we inspire the hope in others that we are creating a community of truthtellers, that we honor the sacredness of the truth, and that we are striving to be Higher Ground Leaders. It represents the signal that others are waiting for—that something better lies ahead. And that is inspiring.

And truth-telling is simple. As Mark Twain said, "If you tell the truth, you don't have to remember anything."

Reflection Ten:
THE CASTLE® PRINCIPLE OF LOVE

Water is fluid, soft, and yielding. But water will wear away rock, which is rigid and cannot yield. As a rule, whatever is fluid, soft, and yielding will overcome whatever is rigid and hard. This is another paradox: what is soft is strong.
—Lao-Tzu

If you don't believe that we should love all others—what exactly do you believe?

If you believe that love is an emotion we reserve only for our loved ones and our very closest friends and is not a "business subject," or something we share with acquaintances, and everyone else, how do you justify that?

> **LOVE**
> Relating to others by touching their hearts in ways that add to who we both are as persons.

Love is to the essential self what oxygen is to the physical self. Love is a noble act that serves others, offering respect, openness, trust, and loyalty. The more we love, the more we tame the social self-part of ourselves, and yet, in doing so, we don't become less in any way, but instead, we become one with those we love.

Love—the Word and the Inspiration

In the Anglo-Saxon tradition, there is a very uneasy relationship with the word love. There are 96 words for love in the Sanskrit-based languages, 80 in Persian, 8 in Greek, and 1 in English. And yet, we all yearn to be loved—even when we are not always easy to love, and even if there are not enough words to describe it. Since the need to be loved is so strong for us all, it is important to realize that we cannot expect to receive what we are not prepared to give. It is through being a loving person that we become an inspiring person.

As Paul McCartney reminds us, "And, in the end, the love you take / Is equal to the love you make."

We are surrounded by inspiring people—they are everywhere—and they are all that way because they choose love over fear and intimidation. Think of those you know who are inspiring—they love you. It is the love within their hearts that inspires you. And they are that way, even when they are feeling personally challenged or just having "a bad day," or when their circumstances might have caused them to be the opposite.

How Love Won in War

In June of 1990, a hotel lobby in Seattle was the scene of an extraordinary meeting between two unique men. Two fighter airplane aces, foes decreed by a war that happened 50 years previously, had flown close enough to each other to allow brief visual contact between them, but they had never actually looked each other in the eye, shaken each other's hand, or, as they were now doing, given each other a big bear hug. There was an immediate, heartfelt rapport between them as they took the elevator up to a room on the third floor to recall the event that was so vividly etched into their minds that one of them still had recurring nightmares about it, and yet the experience still seemed so surreal that they sometimes doubted its occurrence. Settling into the well-upholstered armchairs in the hotel room, and with drinks in hand to facilitate their conversation, they became brothers of choice as they helped each other piece together an incredible puzzle that would tell a remarkable story of chivalry and fear-transcending human love.

On December 20, 1943, a cold and wintry day, Charles L. Brown of the 379th Bomb Group lined up his B-17F for takeoff. He was just 21. Commencing his very first combat mission, he had no awareness about how soon the grace of love would plead with fate to save his life and the lives of his crew members. His plane, whimsically named Ye Olde Pub, was scheduled to take part in the bombing of an FW-190 factory in Bremen, Germany.

As Charlie Brown began his bomb run at 23,000 feet, he immediately encountered heavy and accurate flak as he flew through airstreams registering a frigid minus 60 degrees Fahrenheit. His plane was barraged with a series of severe hits, which knocked out two of its engines, damaged a third, and hobbled his B-17, reducing it to just one engine at full power. The aircraft's compass, controls, oxygen, and hydraulic and electrical systems were all damaged.

177

The pilot and crew received serious wounds, too—a bullet fragment pierced Charlie Brown's right shoulder, while all but one of his comrades were so severely wounded that they could no longer defend themselves or their plane. "They beat us up quite badly," Brown told me. "As I was struggling along, all of a sudden, I looked up and there were eight FW-190s to my right lining up to attack."

As he weighed his rapidly dwindling options, Charlie Brown decided to go on the offensive, using his weakened firepower against the waves of oncoming fighter planes, but, struggling with his injury and starved of oxygen, Brown was unable to sustain his defenses. He remembers becoming inverted after recovering from a steep turn and "looking up" at the ground before passing out. Regaining consciousness, he found the aircraft miraculously flying straight and level, but perilously low—below 1,000 feet.

"When you experience anoxia [a severe deficiency of oxygen in the body]," Brown explained to me, "you have absolutely no memory of what you were doing. The world stops—and it starts. And your memory picks up where the world starts again."

Dropping down from this aerial skirmish, World War II German fighter ace Oberleutnant L. Franz Stigler landed to refuel and rearm when he saw Brown's B-17 emerging from behind a wooded area across the field where he was refueling. Stigler, sensing his third "kill" of the day, sprinted for his plane and jumped into his cockpit, taking off in hot pursuit. Flying at 500 feet above the enemy aircraft, he considered how best to finish it off. "I thought I would do it the classic way, from the rear," remembered Stigler. "So, I flew above and to the rear of the airplane, about 200 feet. I wanted to give his tail-gunner a chance to lift the guns, to point the guns at me. The guns were hanging down."

But the guns didn't lift and Stigler, flying within 20 feet, suddenly realized why. Blood was running down the barrels. "I saw his gunner lying in the back profusely bleeding...so, I couldn't shoot." He then maneuvered alongside the stricken plane's right wing and peered into the cockpit at Brown. "I tried to get him to land in Germany, and he didn't respond at all." Stigler realized that Brown's lack of reaction was due, in part, to his lack of oxygen. As Stigler peered into the aircraft, he could see the crew members frantically treating the wounded and realized that shooting down the aircraft in this condition would be like shooting men in their parachutes. "So, I figured, well, turn him to Sweden, because his airplane was so shot up; I never saw anything flying so shot up."

Though partially dazed, Charlie Brown was concerned for his severely injured comrades on board and therefore rejected the possibility of bailing out or crash-landing. Using the one remaining engine, he edged the battered bomber in a climb, pursuing the risky gamble of reaching the United Kingdom.

And as he did so, glancing out of his right window, he spotted Stigler's Bf-109 (also known as Me-109) flying tight on his wing. Alarmed and struggling to control his badly damaged plane, Brown observed the Bf-109 pilot wave, then fly across the B-17's nose. The pilot signaled for him to land in Germany, but Charlie Brown refused. In an extraordinary act of combat chivalry, the Luftwaffe pilot changed tack, escorting Ye Olde Pub for several miles across the North Sea towards England before saluting, soaring into the grey North Atlantic cloud cover, and returning to continental Europe.

After a harrowing flight across 250 inhospitable miles of the North Sea, Charlie landed his bedraggled bomber safely at Seething, near the English coast.

Who was this mysterious Luftwaffe pilot who gallantly spared Charlie and his comrades? Why had he not completed the mission he had begun, by destroying the plane? These questions would haunt Charles Brown for five decades before they were answered.

After landing, Lieutenant Brown and his crew were debriefed regarding their mission. He was interrogated about his unusual encounter with the Bf-109. This debriefing was classified "secret" and was embargoed for many years. Charles Brown later completed a combat tour, finished college, accepted a regular commission, and served in the Office of Special Investigations with the Joint Chiefs of Staff and in other Air Force and State Department assignments. He retired to Miami, Florida, where he founded an energy conservation and environmental research center specializing in combustion research.

Forty-three years later, Brown decided to unlock his wartime enigma and find the chivalrous Luftwaffe pilot who had spared his plane and the lives of his crew. In 1990, two years after his search began, Charlie Brown received a letter from former Oberleutnant Franz Stigler in response to a notice published in a newsletter for German fighter pilots. Stigler was by then living in Surrey, British Columbia, Canada. Brown called him, and during their phone conversation, the two men compared notes, including time, place, and aircraft markings, and eventually confirmed their extraordinary first meeting in the sky nearly half a century before.

Stigler had enjoyed a celebrated Luftwaffe career: in his 487 combat missions in the Bf-109, he had 28 confirmed victories and was wounded 4 times. He finished the war flying 16 more combat missions in the ME-262 jet, assigned to the select JV-44, the celebrated Squadron of Experts (Aces), making him one of the world's earliest jet fighter pilots in combat. Stigler's decision to spare Charlie Brown's B-17 was even more remarkable considering that in Nazi Germany, such an act would subject Stigler to a court-martial which, if he were found guilty, could have cost him his life. Brown was lucky indeed—previously on that day in December 1943, Stigler had already downed two four-engine bombers and could have earned a Knight's Cross, the highest German Luftwaffe honor, by shooting down one more. But when he saw the human and pitiful condition of the plane and its wounded crew, he felt emotionally unable to carry out the sinister duty required by the rules of war. Instead, he followed the call of love to reprieve, as he would later say, "the most heavily damaged aircraft I ever saw that was still flying."

"Franz came up to within 20 feet of our tail," Brown recalls. "He could see that our tail-gunner was dead, and he could see the blood running down the gun barrels." Stigler later shared with Brown that his decision not to fire at the B-17 was heavily influenced by the fact that, as Brown told me, "He saw men, and he had never fired at men before; he had always fired at airplanes. Not only did he see men, he saw helpless men." Charles Brown believes that Stigler's early training in a monastery from age 8 to 16 was likely a contributing factor to his being able to see the people, rather than just the plane, and allowing compassion and love for fellow humans to guide his action, even though it could have cost him his life.

From their reunion in the Seattle hotel in 1990 until Franz Stigler passed away on March 22, 2008, the two remained close friends. "To say that there was a lot of love between us is an understatement," Brown told me. Stigler's obituary referred to Brown as "special brother Charlie Brown." The online guestbook honoring Stigler contained many entries from people he had never known but who had heard about him and felt compelled to acknowledge this extraordinary Luftwaffe pilot and his selfless act of chivalry and love. One entry read: "Franz...you showed us all that the love for each other we have as human beings is far more powerful than war."

In 2008, more than 60 years after Brown safely landed his badly damaged B-17 on the British coast, wounded crew on board, he was awarded the Air Force Cross, the second highest military decoration that can be awarded to a member of the United States Air Force. Since the time it was first awarded in 1962, there have been less than 200 recipients of this elite medal. But prior to accepting the medal, Brown wanted to ensure recognition for his crew. He nominated each of them for the Silver Star and felt satisfied when the award was granted, even though only three crew members were still alive at the time.

The Mighty Eighth Air Force Museum in Savannah, Georgia, took interest in the decisive encounter between Charlie Brown's B-17 and Franz Stigler's Bf-109, and in 2000, both men met at the museum, commemorating their visit by donating signed lithographs of themselves as World War II pilots. An exhibit at the museum features the encounter as a teaching model in the Character Education programs for the State of Georgia. The Mighty Eighth Air Force Museum is a designated Center for Character Education, in which all students from kindergarten through high school are required to participate. The programs focus on twenty-seven character traits, with "Compassion" being the trait said to have been demonstrated by Franz Stigler in sparing the lives of Charlie Brown and his crew.

In this remarkable story, we learn that at our core, we are not natural killers or warriors. It is hard for us to be brutal or unloving when, as Franz Stigler observed, we see into the faces of real people. It is easier to "kill" a plane than a human spirit. In James Cameron's film *Avatar*, the fictional Na'vi people of the planet Pandora greet each other with the words, "I see you." This is much more than a formality. When they say this to another person, it is an acknowledgement that they see the other as being like themselves, that they honor the sacredness of the other, and the love they have for them, that they understand that they are one, and that what they do to the other, they do to themselves. *Ubuntu* is an Nguni word originating in South Africa, which loosely translates into "a person is a person through other persons." Ubuntu refers to a way of being with other people, behaving well towards them, acting in ways that serve the community, or helping a stranger in need. A person who approaches life in this way is said to *have* ubuntu. He or she is a full person—in other words, a person with love in their heart.

Similarly, the expression *Namaste* holds a special cultural significance in South Asia. In Sanskrit, *nama* means bow; *as* means I; and *te* means you, so, namaste literally means 'bow me you' or 'I bow to you.' It is popularly interpreted as "The divine in me bows to the divine in you," the "divine in you" interpretation coming from the

182

Hindu belief that God resides in everyone. It is a gesture of loving acknowledgment that my soul is one with yours. It acknowledges that the "I" and the "you" that we represent are the same—part of a bigger whole. Even if we find ourselves—metaphorically or literally—embroiled in a violent path that we did not choose, we still have the option of honoring the sacred in the other, and therefore to love them as Franz Stigler and Charlie Brown so clearly demonstrated.

We do not inspire through fear or warrior behavior; we inspire through our loving relationships with, and respect for, others. The mentors, coaches, parents, and teachers who inspired us have all taught us this lesson—they showed their love for us.

Being Strong Enough to Be Gentle

For all our braggadocio, and the legacy of using warrior language, and learning about warrior leadership, and idealizing masculinity and bravado, we are now realizing that greatness and inspiration come from love, not war; from compassion and empathy, not victory, aggression, violence, and domination.

183

In my workshops, I often ask the audience to raise their hands if they agree with this question: "Who would welcome more aggression, machismo, and swagger in their lives?" No one raises their hands. Then I ask, "Who would like more love in their lives?" Everyone raises their hand. I've asked these two questions hundreds of times, and the answers are always the same, confirming that hardly anyone seeks more aggression and almost everyone seeks more love in their lives. Even though this is the inner truth for most of us, we have been socialized to conceal this, and thus, we are hesitant to live it with each other.

Our outdated model of behaving is evolving quickly: the ruthless, macho, show-no-weakness, self-serving beliefs about how we conduct ourselves together are showing themselves to be counter-productive, causing the sicknesses of the soul afflicting our societies. We have a new opportunity to embrace a more enlightened and inspiring way of being—the caring, listening, compassionate person who yearns to make the world a better place and to serve. We can become more conscious individuals who are not afraid to express, and demonstrate, our love for others because it inspires them and everyone else—not least ourselves. It is unnatural for us to live out our lives as pseudo-warriors. We are comprised of the yin and the yang, the feminine as well as the masculine energies, and suppressing the yin at the expense of the yang energy contravenes the desire of the essential self. Fear and violence—the yang energy—can move us to action. But love—the yin energy—inspires.

St. Tomas Aquinas reminds us that "to love is to will the good of the other." How can we not be inspiring if we are living this way? Wouldn't you love anyone who is "willing the good of the other," especially if the "other" is you? If it would affect you so positively in this way, then why would this not happen to others if you "willed the good of others" too? It goes without saying that love is the most powerful emotion of all, and its presence and the sharing of it are utterly inspiring. Equally, the absence of love in our lives is depressing. Which will you choose?

....

Love is the magician that pulls man out of his own hat.

Ben Hecht

....

Reflection Eleven:
THE CASTLE® PRINCIPLE
OF EFFECTIVENESS

People, like nails, lose their effectiveness
when they lose direction and begin to bend.
—Walter Savage Landor

We tend to think of effectiveness as something we *do* to people. But in fact, it is who we *are*, not what we do, that changes the world and people around us. As the Greek author Plutarch wrote, "What we achieve inwardly will change outer reality."

EFFECTIVENESS
Achieving desired
outcomes successfully.

It is important here to distinguish between efficiency and effectiveness. Efficiency is doing things right; effectiveness is doing the right things. We all wish to be effective in our lives. Effectiveness is about reaching the aspirations we have set for ourselves, whether on the spiritual, emotional, mental, or physical levels.

Effectiveness is both a cause and a result. We are the most effective when we have learned to be courageous, authentic, serving, truthful, and loving—when we have fully integrated the first five CASTLE® Principles into our lives and are *living* them. When these attributes have become part of who we are and how we live and inspire others, and if we are following our North Star from that sacred place, Effectiveness is the natural and inevitable consequence. It is inevitable because we are inspired—and therefore inspiring.

185

Inspiration Is the Source
of Exceptional Effectiveness

Inspiration and effectiveness always wax and wane together—both the quality and quantity of output are directly influenced by our level of inspiration at any given time.

Giacomo Puccini said, "Inspiration is an awakening, a quickening of all man's faculties, and it is manifested in all high artistic achievements." And all work is art.

In their peak years, the Beatles were an extraordinarily effective and powerful force. Hardly any sacrifice was too great in their quest for effectiveness—they would sleep in the studio, work through the night—whatever it took to create and record their music and meet studio deadlines. In just one year, for example, 1965, the film *Help* was released, along with 14 songs, including the hits *Help, You've Got to Hide Your Love Away, You're Going to Lose That Girl, Ticket to Ride, I've Just Seen a Face,* and *Yesterday.* But this inspired quartet was in pursuit of their Calling and their year was just warming up. After completing an eleven-date run in the last two weeks of August, including a record-breaking attendance at New York's Shea Stadium, the Beatles wrote and recorded 14 new songs in 30 days for their next album, *Rubber Soul.* Many of these songs, such as *Drive My Car, Norwegian Wood, Nowhere Man, Michelle, Girl, I'm Looking Through You,* and *In My Life,* still stand out as pop classics to this day—more than half a century later—showcasing brilliant levels of creativity and innovation, fresh melodies and lyrics, manipulation of tapes to achieve different or new effects, and novel use of instrumentation, such as the sitar in *Norwegian Wood* and the harpsichord effect in *In My Life.* Before August was over (remember, this was the age of 45 rpm discs), the band had produced two more songs that became a double-sided hit single—*We Can Work It Out* and *Day*

Tripper. Sixteen recorded and published songs in 30 days! And their pursuit of effectiveness—the quest for *exactly* the result they were looking for, knew no bounds. To get their song *I Will* just right, the Beatles recorded it 65 times.

The beating heart of effectiveness is the inspiration that comes from a deep inner awareness of one's Why-Be-Do®—our North Star—tempered by the CASTLE® Principles and a prodigious commitment to mastery. This effectiveness, at its very highest levels, is sometimes referred to as genius. But as Buckminster Fuller reminded us, "Everyone is born a genius, but the process of living de-geniuses them." The Beatles were a remarkable example of The Optimum Potential Theory described in Reflection Three.

Positive, Inspiring, Simple, Elegant, and Graceful—The Essentials of Effectiveness

The beautiful thing about all this is that it requires no contrary effort—no effort that requires us to "push against" something—just the wisdom to follow the natural energy of what we know to be right. And it will work best for us when we listen—truly listen—to our inner voices, our essential selves, and follow the (sometimes counterintuitive) paths we are being asked to take: what we earlier defined as authenticity. The path to effectiveness is straightforward, logical, elegant, and graceful. I have summarized and defined the essentials of effectiveness as follows:

- There is nothing to learn, only old habits to break (unlearning) and original qualities to restore.
- There is nothing complicated here—it is so *simple* that it is almost absurd. Remember, the word being used here is *simple*—and that does not necessarily mean *easy*. Think of the phone as a metaphor—it is a perfect example of the

complex made simple. Just 10 digits will connect you to your friend in Timbuktu, but the science of how that happens is not easy. It is effective because you do not have to be concerned with the complexity—the result is simplicity, which is effective.

- The old adage is, "If it ain't broke, don't fix it." But in this case, the opposite is more likely to be true: if it feels boring, not fun, or it is not working as effectively as it could, then it may be time to retire the old model or belief and replace it with a new one.

- If it is negative in any way—ugly, dirty, noisy, unappealing, complicated, harmful, hurtful, dangerous, environmentally destructive, or dishonest—it is bound to fail. This is so because negative energy is a signal that we are forcing something unnaturally.

- If it is *elegant and graceful*, it is bound to succeed, because the default center point of life, and a key source of inspiration, rests in elegance and grace, which leads to effectiveness.

- Learning, followed by constant practice, leads to mastery, which results in effectiveness.

- Focus and mental preparation are essential for effectiveness.

- An open mindset prepares the ground for effectiveness.

- If it is uninspiring, it is going to be harder to achieve; make it *inspiring*, and the natural energy towards completion will flow your way, making it effective.

- Visualizing successful outcomes leads to effectiveness.

- If it affronts the essential self, it will fail. Honor the sacredness of the other, respect the concept of oneness, then alignment of interests and purpose will follow, and it will be effective.

As we have seen, we must first be inspired before we can be effective. Effectiveness is facilitated by courage, because being effective requires that we invest more than a mediocre effort—more than merely what we can get away with, and that often requires courage. It requires our highest levels of commitment.

Effectiveness Lessons from a Rock Climber

Many say that John Bachar was the greatest solo climber of all time. Most climbers use ropes, bolts, and pitons in their ascents, rappelling down the mountain using lines. John Bachar raised the bar for all climbers by eschewing all of these aids in a form known as free climbing or free soloing. His climbing style and courage were legendary, and he became a mythical and charismatic figure to many. He climbed shiny granite vertical walls like a spider, or, as he preferred to describe it, like a starfish. He moved very deliberately, almost in slow motion, placing a careful handgrip here, raising his leg parallel to his hip to a rim of rock there, hauling his body up with one arm, and repeating this balletic routine until he reached his destination. Unlike many mountaineers, he felt no urge to "conquer" the rock face, and getting to the top was not the point. What counted for John Bachar were the elegance, grace, and control of how he got there—as described in *The Essentials of Effectiveness* above.

Was he afraid of falling? By his own admission, he was terrified of heights, but he overcame these fears—thus becoming more effective—by practicing his moves first on boulders, from which he could fall five feet onto sand, and eventually working up to greater heights, until he could confidently climb up several hundred feet calmly with

189

his palms open and relaxed, as if he were walking to the store. As he observed, we can walk on a line on the ground with no problem, but as soon as we place the same line on top of a building, we lose our confidence, and therefore our effectiveness. Confidence was a key word for John Bachar—and confidence is the product of courage, which leads to greater effectiveness. Did he dare look down? "Of course. It's beautiful up there." Besides, he added, "Just looking down isn't going to kill you." He knew the risks associated with free soloing were the price exacted by his passion for it.

Goethe wrote, "Knowing is not enough; we must apply. Willing is not enough; we must do." Yoda put it another way, "Do. Or do not. There is no try." In order to maintain his courage, confidence, and effectiveness, John Bachar practiced and worked out two hours every day, perfecting his technique and honing the strength upon which his life would depend. At Camp IV in Yosemite, he built his own gym among the trees, in which he and his fellow pony-tailed idealists trained to be "masters of stone." They tied ropes to trees to practice tightrope-walking in order to enhance their balance and built hanging ladders that became known as Bachar ladders. He followed a strict nutritional regimen. His life was an evolution of courage, inspiration, commitment, and effectiveness: at 14, he was a weakling who could do only two pull-ups; at 16, when he made his first free ascent at Joshua Tree, he could do 27. By his mid-twenties, he had mastered doing pull-ups with one arm, or with 140 lbs. of weights. At his peak, Bachar was able to perform a one-arm pull-up with 12.5 lbs. of weight in his other hand.

He would seem to grasp what appeared to be nothing—placing the special boots, made by his own company, on a mere blemish in the rock, a "smear," or a hairline crack, sometimes less than half an inch wide, suddenly freeing both arms from the rock to make a lunge to the next handhold. More than 50 feet up, one mistake could spell death, and he was often on faces of 200 feet or more above ground.

Effectiveness also comes from focus and mental preparation. Bachar's training regimen was both mental and physical. The superior caliber of personal focus required to achieve exceptional levels of effectiveness is realized through learning how to simultaneously relax and concentrate. Many achieve this through the practice of meditation. Bachar's technique was to visualize nothing except the "little circle of rock" ahead of him and emptying his mind of everything except the fluidity and perfection of his moves—in a way, his own form of meditation. If he required a surge of strength, he visualized throwing an electric switch to flood his muscles with power. He imagined his fingers to be steel hooks and himself as a dancer. His climbing was the opposite of reckless—he was a mathematician who was the son of a mathematician; at UCLA he majored in math prior to becoming a climber. Each mission up a polished granite tower was, for him, an act of analysis. Before each ascent, he would mentally divide each boulder problem into sections, and prepare his mental state according to three zones: zone 1, no harm if he fell; zone 2, hospital, but he'd survive; zone 3, death if he made a mistake.

It was better to backtrack, every move executed with elegance and grace in reverse, than to climb in a clumsy or clunky way. It was better, he said, to be a flawless failure than a mediocre success.

On July 5, 2009, John Bachar died while climbing alone at the Dike Wall near Mammoth Lakes in the eastern Sierra, near his home in California. He was 52, and until that fateful day, a bruised back had been his worst injury. He escaped many close calls, and each time, he believed, the rock had merely let him get away with it. The rock was his superior and, he felt, should remain as if it had never been climbed.

John Bachar's death did not make him a failure because the legacy he left was a string of firsts—ascents, challenges, and breakthroughs—in addition to his many protégés. Another legendary climber, John Long, observed, "There has never been anyone like John Bachar, and there never will be again." And Peter Croft, with whom Bachar made a one-mile vertical ascent in less than 14 hours, said, "Yosemite was *the* place, Bachar was *the* guy; that makes him more than just a climber."

Effectiveness is always personal. Effective families, groups, and teams are only effective if their individual members are effective. That is why we concentrate on the practice of effectiveness at the individual level. Bachar was a classic example.

In fact, anything we choose to do well, such as being an inspiration for others or achieving mastery, requires, as John Bachar demonstrated, great commitment—and great commitment leads to effectiveness.

The Trim Tab—Effectiveness is the Sum of Many Small Actions

Sometimes, we have a tendency to think small, as if the world were too big for it to be affected by our puny efforts. Such thinking is the enemy of effectiveness because it is often self-fulfilling. We are not small or insignificant, but powerful beyond our imagination. Buckminster Fuller, famed architect, author, designer, futurist, inventor, and visionary, said, "I always say to myself: What is the most important thing we can think about at this extraordinary moment?" In an interview with Barry Farrel, Buckminster Fuller said, "Something hit me very hard once, thinking about what one little man could do. Think of the Queen Mary—the whole ship goes by and then comes the rudder. And there's a tiny thing at the edge of the rudder called a trim tab. It's a miniature rudder. Just moving the little trim tab builds a low pressure that pulls the rudder around. Takes almost no effort at all. So I said that the little individual can be a trim tab. Society thinks it's going right by you, that it's left you altogether. But if you're doing dynamic things mentally, the fact is that you can just put your foot out like that and the whole big ship of state is going to go. So I said, 'Call me Trimtab.'"

In the period leading up to his death, Buckminster Fuller's wife had been lying comatose in a Los Angeles hospital, dying of cancer. It was while visiting her there that he exclaimed, at a certain point: "She is squeezing my hand!" He then stood up, suffered a heart attack, and died an hour later. Chiseled into Buckminster Fuller's gravestone at Cambridge, Massachusetts, are the words: *Call me Trimtab.*

193

Unlearning Is a Precondition for Effectiveness

Many people find it hard to believe that making a breakthrough that leads to a significant increase in effectiveness can be achieved quickly. People often take me aside and quietly ask me to share the "secret sauce" that I teach clients—in skiing, personal development, and in coaching and leadership. But, in all these environments, I tell them, "You're asking the wrong question. You see, it's not so much about what we need to learn; it's more about what we need to *unlearn.*"

On February 12, 1995, the *New York Times* broke a story about the Swedish government's embarrassing admission that their defense forces had been blowing up minks and seals instead of Russian submarines in their coastal waters. The *Times* quoted then-Prime Minister Ingvar Carlsson as saying, "It's a sad fact that what was originally stated to be intrusions into our waters, have proved to be minks."

Beginning in the mid-1970s—the hair-trigger, paranoid, cold-war years—the Swedish defense forces began hunting submarines in the fjords and islands of Sweden, Norway, and Finland, a sensitive buffer zone between the former communist Soviet Union and the West. Depth charges and grenades were dropped, and remote-controlled mines detonated in dozens of forays each year—always during the warmer months. A spokesperson reported that, on one occasion, "the prowler was detected and trapped in 282 feet of water... about 60 miles south of Stockholm," but, as in every other case, the submarines evaded their pursuers, slipping away amidst the ensuing confusion and turbulence.[40] In October 1981, Swedish suspicions were augmented when a Soviet submarine made a navigation error, becoming stranded on rocks near a military base at Karlskrona. The submarine was a diesel-powered vessel of the type called Whiskey class by NATO.

Many theories abounded: the Soviets were seeking hiding places for future warfare; the Soviets were testing their submarines' evasion techniques; the Soviets were probing Swedish antisubmarine defenses. The repeated denials by the Soviets of their submarines' presence in Swedish territorial waters simply heightened the Swedes' suspicions. In 1982, Rear Admiral Per Rudbeck declared, "a foreign power is preparing for war against us."

In February of 1995, Owe Wiktorin, Supreme Commander of Sweden's armed services, revealed Sweden's faux pas while presenting a report about his country's military and naval activity. He said that through the use of new hydrophonic measuring instruments, it had

---

40 Starbuck, William, H., "Unlearning Ineffective Behavior or Obsolete Technologies," *International Journal of Technology Management*, 1996, 11: 725-737; and *The New York Times*, Sunday, February 12, 1995, section 1, page 10, New York edition

been shown that sounds that had long been identified as coming from foreign submarines could actually be traced to minks, which had similar sound patterns. He concluded that, since 1992 at least, there had been no intrusions by Soviet submarines into Sweden's territorial waters.

Even though the possibility that the Swedish Navy might be pursuing playful minks and seals had been suggested as early as 1987, the Swedish military brass had fallen back on their old knowledge, beliefs, and detection techniques—a failure to unlearn. When Tero Harkonen, a Swedish seal expert, first suggested that the Navy's antisubmarine response had been tripped by young seals playing, his findings were dismissed. "They can play, gush through the water, and even create foam on the surface," he tried to explain, but navy officials insisted that they had seen the bubbles of divers and had corralled a foreign mini-submarine or another type of underwater vessel with their nets. They justified their erroneous assessment by pointing to the many "reliable" sightings of suspected alien submarines and submarine activity in the area over the preceding two months. Even after the mink-and-seal theory was raised, the Swedish Navy continued searching and dropping depth charges for ten more days before abandoning the exercises. *Facts do not cease to exist because they are ignored.* The tendency to ignore information and resisting the opportunity to learn works against effectiveness.

195

Knowers and Learners

We can view people as largely falling into two distinct categories: knowers and learners. Knowers are cynical and closed. Learners are curious and inspired by their learning. Knowers tend to let you know that they know everything already—you will hear them frequently say, "I know." They tend to have a fixed mindset which closes them to new ideas, options, and learning. It is difficult to teach a new idea to a person whose mind is already made up. As Shunryu Suzuki reminds us, "If your mind is empty, it is always ready for anything, it is open to everything. In the beginner's mind there are many possibilities, but in the expert's mind there are few."

A story is told about Nan-in, a Japanese Zen master during the Meiji era (1868–1912), who received a university professor who came to learn about Zen. As Nan-in served him tea, he poured the visitor's cup until it was full, and then continued pouring.

The professor watched the overflow until he could no longer constrain himself. "The teacup is overflowing. There is no room for any more."

"Like this cup," Nin-in said, "you are full of your own opinions and speculations. How can I show you Zen unless you first empty your cup?"[41]

Effectiveness is enabled through an open mind. When we are frightened, or when we begin calcifying our beliefs or attitudes, or have a certainty about the correctness of our knowledge, we resort to the familiar, and close our minds. When this happens, new learning is impossible, and effectiveness is seriously impaired. An intermediate skier, faced with a cliff and a 60-degree pitch, will resort to old, defensive habits—a *snow plow* (a maneuver in which the skis are wedged to slow down speed) or *side-slipping* (a technique where the skis are angled at 90 degrees to the incline of the slope to slow or avert descent). Defensive approaches are chosen when we experience fear. Advanced skiers, on the other hand, would approach such a challenge by choosing *offensive* techniques based on courage and commitment. They would also be more likely to ask a more experi-

---

41 Zen Flesh, Zen Bones: A Collection of Zen and Pre-Zen Writings, by Paul Reps and Nyogen Senzaki, Tuttle Publishing; 1998

enced skier for advice. In doing so, they are able to easily set aside old methods and habits, and this is easy to do with a trusted teacher—someone who can inspire the confidence required to overcome the fear associated with the challenge. At first glance, skiing down the cliff may seem daunting. However, if the descent is broken into three pieces—tight turns for the first and steepest third, wider turns for the less steep middle third, and carving turns for the ski-out, for example, it becomes manageable. In my retreats, I have found that the easy part is teaching the skills necessary for a safe descent; the really hard part is ensuring that the student is prepared to let go of old ideas, such as the snow plow. And teaching the necessary skills cannot happen until a commitment is made by the student to let go of a system and a set of beliefs they have been using for most of their lives—emptying the mind. Teaching the skills necessary for the descent is easy; getting the student to let go of old techniques, especially the long-embraced snow plow, is the hard part. And so it is in life.

197

Learners have a different mindset. In their minds, nothing is fixed, everything is open to revision, information updates are frequent, and currency and relevance result. Learners keep growing—knowers stopped growing long ago. Learners are constantly inspired by the fresh things they do or ideas they discover. Knowers are bored and defensive when presented with information that challenges what they think they already know. Learners are always ready to try something new, new foods, art, music, ideas, beliefs, locations, friends, hobbies, work opportunities—and so they are constantly being inspired by the freshness of their discoveries. Knowers, on the other hand, are hard to inspire, and often fail to be inspiring, because they are cynical and apathetic, and tend to be jaded about things that do not fit neatly into their existing worldview. Lionel Suggs advises us, "The secrets of the universe aren't really secrets. It's just that humanity is too subjugated by their blissful ignorance to ask the right questions. When you have all of the answers, but are unable to ask any questions to them, then all you have are secrets."

In Part One, we reviewed the concepts of a "growth mindset" and a "fixed mindset." Unlearning and a growth, or open, mindset is a prerequisite for effectiveness, which leads to growth. We see the world not as it is, but as we would like it to be, and as we have experienced it, and unlearning and openness is like seeing the world with new eyes. As Marcel Proust said, "The real voyage of discovery consists, not in seeking new landscapes, but in having new eyes"— being a learner.

The steps to unlearning, opening the mind, letting go and becoming more effective are:

1. Admit that an old practice, belief, or attitude is not solving the current challenge and is no longer serving you, and therefore doing more of it will not lead to the desired outcomes.

2. Open your mind. Pause your tendency to prejudge. Carl Jung said, "Thinking is difficult, that's why most people judge." Yield to the view that there are alternatives to the way you have "always done it" until now.

3. Switch from trying to rationalize the use of your long-favored solution to asking questions about how you can change, learn, and grow. Learners ask questions; knowers have answers.

4. Commit to terminating the old way—forever. This is the toughest part.

5. Practice and perfect the new way. This is the easiest part.

That's the "secret sauce." As Satchel Paige said, "It's not what you don't know that hurts you; it's what you know that just ain't so."

Letting Go of Old Ideas—Two Parables

Two monks who were traveling together decided to rest by a river.

Soon, a young woman arrived, and wary of the current, she asked if they would be kind enough to carry her across.

One of the monks hesitated, but the other quickly picked her up onto his shoulders, transported her across the water, and gently lowered her onto the ground on the other side of the river. She thanked him for his kindness and departed.

As the monks continued on their way, the one was brooding and thoughtful. Unable to contain himself any further, he spoke out. "Brother, our spiritual training teaches us to avoid any contact with women, but you picked that one up on your shoulders and carried her!"

"Brother," the second monk replied, "I set her down on the other side, while you are still carrying her."

Letting go of old ideas is perhaps the most formidable barriers to change and becoming inspired and inspiring.

A wise farmer owned a prize horse, but one day it ran away. The neighbors came to see him and commiserate. "Isn't it a terrible thing that your horse ran away?" they all said.

The farmer said, "Maybe yes, maybe no."

The next day, the horse returned, with a filly in tow. The neighbors came to visit again and declared, "How lucky you are that that your horse came back and brought a beautiful filly with him?"

The farmer said, "Maybe yes, maybe no."

The next day, the farmer's son was training the filly, but when it threw him, he fell and broke his leg. Once again the neighbors offered up their opinion, "Isn't it a tragedy that your son broke his leg?

Now he can't help you with your farming projects until he is well again. That's just a shame!"

The farmer said, "Maybe yes, maybe no."

The next day, the Emperor paid an unexpected visit to conscript all the young men for his latest war. But because the farmer's son's leg was broken, they allowed him to remain on the farm. The neighbors, ever ready to pass judgment said, "How fortunate that your son had a broken leg. This saved him from having to risk his life in the war!"

The farmer said, "Maybe yes, maybe no..."

How we see things depends upon our experience, our habits of perception (negative, positive, cynical, optimistic, etc.) and, most of all, our choices. We can hand over choice to fate or take control and choose intentionally. If we tend to be cynical, then this is the message that becomes our mental model, our frame, through which we perceive ideas, communications, experiences—life. We then convert this into our reality. But if we choose to "reframe"—that is, delete the existing frame from our mind, and replace it with a different frame—we immediately alter our perception, our physical, mental, and spiritual states, and our behavior and future actions. Being effective depends, very often, on reframing. Let me give you an example:

One of our health-care clients operates a very successful cardiology department. It has high volumes, significant revenues, and is one of the hospital's most profitable divisions. The old "frame" positioned this business as "the heart unit" which, to most of their team, meant providing appropriate surgical procedures for patients suffering from various heart ailments, and for many years, this was a very successful philosophy. One day, they reframed their view of this business unit by proposing the creative idea of establishing a health club. They reasoned that a health club could be reframed as an extension of the heart unit: if patients followed good exercise and nutrition regimens, they would remain healthy—a goal shared by the heart unit. By integrating the two, they could expand their customer base—revenues would be generated either way—from paying customers of the health club, or from the surgeries conducted in the cardiology department. If members of the health club failed to show up or practice the healthy lifestyles being taught at the health club, they might end up in the other business unit owned by the same organization—the cardiology department. Eventually, their new health club grew to 20,000 members and was a runaway success, and resulted in the cardiology department successfully generating two separate income streams.

This creative and inspired leadership team continued to reframe as they sought greater effectiveness. Because their health club was now so successful as an extension of their cardiology unit, they began to receive visitors from other healthcare systems from around the country who wanted to learn from them. This caused them to realize that there was an opportunity to franchise their system to other healthcare facilities across the nation. So, they wrote programs that could be taught to others, including their procedures, developing a launch plan, designing a club, selecting and purchasing equipment, hiring and training staff, and marketing. In doing so, and by being learners, they created a third business of franchising their proprietary processes—which also became part of the cardiology unit. All this was achieved by frequently reframing what they saw, staying in an open, learner's mindset, and reinterpreting new data as it appeared into more effective business practices.

201

Effective people reframe regularly, refusing to accept the status quo, always searching for a new way of seeing things—which others find inspiring—and therefore increasing their effectiveness. Are you reframing frequently to accelerate your effectiveness?

Collaborating for Effectiveness

Competitiveness is the principal doctrine and default behavior guiding many people's lives. It underpins business, politics, sports, academia, and many other fields. But unlearning this limbic addiction and replacing it with collaboration—the honoring of other souls—is another example of the potential available to us to be more effective. If we are prepared to unlearn old established ideas and become more open to considering new thinking, an entire new world is available to us. I don't mean to infer that everything old is "bad," but I am suggesting that we would do well to compare new ideas with old ones and choose the most effective option.

Effectiveness through Forgiveness

Eldon Taylor wrote, "When you forgive, you essentially undo the ability to blame. If there is nothing to blame, then you are in charge of your response to outside stimuli. There is less room for anger without blame. There is less to fear when you're empowered." The inability to forgive impairs our effectiveness. Our emotions can cloud our judgment, resulting in emotional decisions that result in ineffectiveness.

Effectiveness requires objectivity. If we have been betrayed or hurt by another, any resulting anger, feelings of revenge, sense of woundedness, spite, bruised social self, or shadow behavior will lower our effectiveness. These emotions cloud our judgment. Forgiveness not only removes this clutter from our perspective, it also transforms the other person by encouraging them to recreate a relationship, and relationships that are whole and inspiring are essential to effectiveness.

Forgiveness is not simply an act of altruism. It is a form of enlightened self-interest that leads to effectiveness. It is the removal of anger, which is an obstacle to effectiveness. Forgiveness warms the heart and cools the pain. When we fail to forgive, we drink the same poison that we are giving others. Mark Twain reminds us that "Forgiveness is the fragrance that the violet sheds on the heel that crushed it." I have worked with many family and business groups and teams where individual members have been wronged by each other, sometimes long ago, and the grudge remains as an aggravation that is massaged daily. Carrying a grudge is a heavy burden. Ugly things are said about and done to each other, which significantly lowers the effectiveness of a family or a team. After all, if we aspire to be a member of a high-functioning team—at home, or at work—how can this be achieved when those who are essential to each other's success are throwing boulders in front of each other?

What is required here are reconciliation and forgiveness. Without these, we cannot move on, or achieve something great, and the situation will remain uninspiring for both the victim and persecutor—even worse, it will drain the energy from all involved.

Forgiveness is a commitment to letting go of anger, resentment, and revenge. Resentment towards another is a negative-energy chord that connects you to them and keeps you bound until you decide to melt that destructive bond with forgiveness. Anger makes one smaller; forgiveness helps you to grow and become more effective. The benefit of forgiveness is often greater for the person who forgives than for the one who is being forgiven—forgiveness sets a prisoner free, and often that prisoner is you. Our role in life is to act as coach, mentor, arbitrator, broker, and healer with any family, friends, or

203

work colleagues who remain unwilling to forgive. No one can be effective—or whole—where forgiveness still waits outside the door.

Growing the Young People Who Will Run Our World

I have often marveled at the frequency and persistence of dysfunctional behaviors among families and organizations—and even friends. This has caused me to reflect deeply on how we teach young people. How could we do this more effectively in our educational system, because, it seems to me, if we were more effective at teaching values and how to be an inspiring human in our schools, the quality of the young adults that emerge and grow into those who lead and manage our world, might be greater. It seems a reasonable proposition that if we were to invest in significantly increasing the learning for students, enabling them to become inspiring human beings while at school, they might bring this awareness and practice more broadly into their later lives. The ideal sequence of this learning process is to first teach students how to become inspired—a topic that is absent from most levels of education—and later how to be an inspiring person for others.

We have transformed our education system of the last few decades from one that educates students to live inspiring lives to one that teaches them how to find jobs. The issues facing young people as they begin their adult lives, and for which we have no teaching curriculum, in chronological order, are:

1. Dealing with death—early in the child's life, someone very close to them dies—an experience for which they are totally unprepared
2. Building relationships
3. Finding a Calling

4. Finding a soulmate
5. Buying a house
6. Raising children
7. Financial literacy
8. How to lead
9. Nutrition, health, and well-being

If we want our young people to live effective lives, with meaning, fulfillment, and purpose, these are some of the key life skills we should be teaching, and if the schools cannot do so, then we as parents must first learn these, and then teach them.

How would our educational systems become more effective, and how would students benefit, if the values inherent in the CASTLE® Principles were incorporated into the culture of our schools and universities? North Gwinnett High School in the town of Suwanee near Atlanta, Georgia, is one of six schools in the North Gwinnett Cluster and part of the Gwinnett County Public Schools system—the 13th largest school district in the United States. Founded in 1958, the school has grown to become one of the leading schools in Gwinnett County and in the state of Georgia. With a teaching staff of almost 250, the school currently serves some 3,000 students.

In 2007, the school's then-principal, John Green, read about the CASTLE® Principles in my book *ONE: The Art and Practice of Conscious Leadership* and realized that they would be a perfect complement to the leadership program he had initiated at North Gwinnett three years earlier based on the concepts of "lead yourself, lead your club or team, lead your school and community, lead your life." He felt that the CASTLE® Principles fit perfectly with the school's vision that "*all* students are leaders, all students add value," and they could help to dispel the misperception that leadership is positional or hierarchical. Green shared this discovery with a colleague, Nancy Ward, who ran the Gwinnett County Student Leadership Team, and jointly they made the decision to introduce students to the CASTLE® Principles. In a Fall retreat with the school's student leaders that year, Green based his presentation, which he titled "Leadership Mindset," on the CASTLE® Principles.

Since then, the CASTLE® Principles have been absorbed into the culture and student leadership programs at North Gwinnett, alongside other leadership teachings of similar orientation. "The CASTLE® Principles have served as a way to generate common language for our teacher-leaders and school leaders," says Green. "They represent a sort of integrative curriculum, pre-K through grade 12, because they can easily be understood by students at all levels, some even by five-year-olds. *Every* kid can do something to help another student, or to help someone else."

The concept of servant-leadership, and the notion of being other-focused, is deeply ingrained in the school's culture. The slogan "It's not all about me" serves as the cultural description of North Gwinnett's school community. And its transforming effects are immediately noticeable to others. When Ed Shaddix assumed the school's leadership, taking over from John Green, who was promoted to area superintendent after ten years as principal, he quickly realized that this school was unlike any other he had ever been part of. It became obvious to him that his predecessor had built, as Shaddix says, "an unbelievable administrative team with high levels of trust and capability." At North Gwinnett, leadership was not just talked about—it was *lived*.

"Leadership is a huge component of the culture here," says Shaddix. "There is an expectation of behavior that the kids set for themselves, and that the community sets for them, that you don't find anywhere else. Everyone works in an atmosphere of mutual respect, and we hold the expectation that all students can learn at high levels. Our teachers believe it, our kids believe it, and our results prove it."

According to *Newsweek* magazine's "Top Public High Schools," North Gwinnett ranked number one in Gwinnett County and number 212 in America following the introduction of the CASTLE® Principles, up from 682 four years earlier. The school's remarkable academic results support North Gwinnett's reputation as a model for other schools in the county and the state of Georgia, with 90 percent of graduating seniors attending post-secondary schools, and 46 percent of seniors receiving a total of more than $10 million in scholarships offered. In the year following the introduction of CASTLE® Principles, 65 percent of North Gwinnett's seniors had scored a "3 or better" on an advanced placement exam while in high school, which translates into two-thirds of the school's seniors having started college with at least one course credit earned in the advanced placement program. This figure is significantly above the state average of 25 percent.

Building on the strong foundation established by his predecessor, Ed Shaddix implemented an effective tutoring system run by the school's students. In addition to helping each other—modeling the CASTLE® Principle of Service—North Gwinnett's students serve as mentors to the younger students in the elementary and middle schools that feed into North Gwinnett.

Inspired by the same spirit of mentoring and servant-leadership, the administrative team at North Gwinnett offers assistance to other schools in the district and beyond. The school receives many visitors each year, often principals from other schools, who come to learn about its unique culture and academic environment. "We'd like for as many schools as possible to realize that once you adopt the philosophy of the CASTLE® Principles, that all students can be leaders," says John Green, "and that when you believe this, it can make a huge difference in what your students produce in terms of their work and how productive they become once they leave school and go on to college, and whatever it is they go on to do."

When asked how utilizing the CASTLE® Principles had contributed to North Gwinnett's effectiveness, John Green shared a revealing insight: "Just as *Effectiveness* is the last letter in the CASTLE® Principles, so it also provides the validation for what you've done utilizing the other CASTLE® Principles. You can't help but be effective if you practice Courage, Authenticity, Service, Truthfulness, and Love. And so Effectiveness becomes a validation component. I also see it as being multidimensional, where, for instance, the more love you can develop, the more effective you are. And while we need to recognize the unique value of each of the CASTLE® Principles in terms of its contribution to overall effectiveness, it's important to recognize that they are all interconnected and working as one."

North Gwinnett is a model of Effectiveness and all six CASTLE® Principles in action, and also for the possibilities of how we could change the world, making it more inspiring, by introducing these ideas into our primary education system.

The Circular Logic of the CASTLE® Principles

You will recall that we described earlier how the CASTLE® Principles were first discovered, by learning what people did NOT like about others. For example, living the opposites of the CASTLE® Principles—in cowardice, phoniness, selfishness, lying, and fear—

we become ineffective. It's easy to see how this all comes together, isn't it? The opposite is also true—effectiveness comes from courage, authenticity, service, truthfulness, and love. Just as courage is the first of the CASTLE® Principles, because all of the others can then follow, so effectiveness is the last one, because all the others lead to it.

It takes the effort of negative energy, which can only come from the social self, to oppose the CASTLE® Principles—to be cowardly, duplicitous, selfish, dishonest, aggressive, or incompetent, and especially to be profane. And the opposite is true—pouring our energy into being courageous, authentic, serving, truthful, loving, and effective yields the outcomes, inspiration, and the sacredness we yearn for. Pouring our energy into the clarity and purity of our Why-Be-Do® is also the most effective way to live our lives and get things done.

This applies to all the CASTLE® Principles. We call this the Circular Logic of the CASTLE® Principles, because they are all interconnected—they are ONE, as John Green has explained. We teach and learn the CASTLE® Principles by pulling them apart from each other and studying them one at a time. This is a Western methodology of teaching. But this is not the way we *live* them. I suspect that Mother Teresa *lived* the CASTLE® Principles, even though she had probably never heard of them. Like a giant emotional and spiritual hologram, every part is interconnected with every other part. Thus, one CASTLE® Principle will be accomplished only through the engagement of the others. Understanding this is essential to effectiveness. We will be effective when we become the other five CASTLE® Principles, and we become the other five CASTLE® Principles by being effective. Using the CASTLE® Principle of Effectiveness, as an example, the following summary describes this phenomenon:

- **Courage:** I cannot become effective unless I am first courageous. Because everything is initiated through courage, strengthening my effectiveness cannot happen until I have the courage to do what is necessary to be more effective. But the reverse is also true: I will be courageous when I choose to live in a fully effective way. The greater my courage, the greater my effectiveness. Courage and effectiveness are ONE.

- **Authenticity**: Inauthenticity is an inefficient use of energy. Authenticity is the transparent and effective use of all resources. When I am authentic, I build trust, and when I build trust, I create stronger relationships, which lead to greater effectiveness. I will be effective when I see the power and utility of authenticity.

- **Service**: To be effective, I must serve—effectiveness without a serving purpose is pointless. Unless you and I, and the larger community, are being served, service is not effective. Like engines, we deteriorate, or become ineffective, if we are not maintained (or serviced). I will serve others, such as my family, friends or organization, best when I first live in a fully effective way. And I will be most effective when I ensure that all my actions are serving others.

- **Truthfulness**: Telling the truth requires little effort; lying requires considerable negative energy. The truth exists; lies are constructed. Lying is never effective, and when it is discovered, all advantage is lost. A lie always leads to betrayal, and betrayal always leads to a loss of trust. And effectiveness cannot be built without trust. I will be truthful when I practice the effectiveness of living truthfully.

- **Love**: If we can be as successful as we are by living as warriors, imagine how effective we could be by living in a loving and compassionate way. We would lose the toxicity, but none of the advantages, while gaining all the benefits that loving, empathetic relationships can generate. Warriors destroy and dominate, creating fear and motivating with power. Leaders with a loving heart inspire others to greater effectiveness because everyone grows and thrives and no one dies. I will be fully loving when I commit to living in a fully effective way. And I will be most effective when I am a loving human being.

The same argument can be made for any of the CASTLE® Principles. Take Truthfulness, for example: Truthfulness requires courage, it is also authentic, it serves others, it is a loving thing to do and it is effective. We teach the CASTLE® Principles as six independent ideas, but in reality they are interdependent and co-dependent—one will not work as well as it could without the others.

The CASTLE® Principles are remarkably "sticky." I have met people who have said to me that they heard me speak at a conference twenty years ago. When I ask them if they remember what I spoke about at that time, they quickly reply, "The CASTLE® Principles—I still live them every day!" That speaks to the power of these six simple ways of living that inspire others. The reason, as we have reviewed earlier, is that they are already within us, and thus there is nothing to learn—just six principles to recover, polish, and practice. Once you embrace, and start living, the CASTLE® Principles, they will become a part of who you are and stay with you for the rest of your life. Although Mahatma Gandhi may have lived the CASTLE® Principles without ever having heard of them, he didn't need to—it was just deeply engrained in his way of being, and, in time, so it will be with you.

....

Ineffective people live day after day with unused potential.

Steven Covey

....

PART FOUR

The Torch— Inspiring the World

Part Four
The Torch:
Inspiring The World

● ● ●

We're here for a reason. I believe a bit of the reason is to throw little torches out to lead people through the dark.
—Whoopi Goldberg

The spark ignites the flame, and the flame sets fire to the torch. We convert the spark into a flame, using it to light the torch, which we pass to others. The torch is the legacy we create; it is the gift of mentoring, coaching, and supporting people's growth so that their spark is awakened. The torch is paying it forward, teaching others, helping them to develop, and sharing the philosophy of being inspiring with them. And when we light another's torch, our own flame is never diminished. On the contrary, it burns even more brightly. Albert Schweitzer reminds us that, "In everyone's life, at some time, our inner fire goes out. It is then burst into flame by an encounter with another human being. We should all be thankful for those people who rekindle the inner spirit." That is our role as inspiring beings, and how we change the world.

Reflection Twelve:
GUIDING OTHERS TO GREATNESS

*We can choose to make the success of all humanity our
personal business. We can choose to be audacious enough
to take responsibility for the entire human family.
We can choose to make our love for the World what our
lives are really about. Each of us now has the opportunity,
the privilege to make a difference in creating a World
that works for all of us. It will require courage, audacity
and heart. It is much more radical than a revolution,
it is the beginning of a transformation in the quality of life on
our planet. You have the power to fire a shot heard around the
World. If not you, who? If not here, where? If not now, when?*

—Werner Erhard

Paying It Forward

The torch represents our role as teachers, guides, coaches, leaders, helpers, and supporters for others. As teachers lighting the flame for others with our torch, we will do well to remember William Arthur's advice: "The mediocre teacher tells. The good teacher explains. The superior teacher demonstrates. The great teacher inspires." Being inspired and inspiring others carries with it the responsibility to share what we have learned—to pay it forward. In a letter accompanying a financial gift to a friend, Benjamin Franklin wrote, "I do not pretend to *give* such a Sum; I only *lend* it to you. When you shall return to your country with a good character, you cannot fail of getting into some business that will in time enable you to pay all your debts. In that case, when you meet with another honest man in similar distress, you must pay me by lending this Sum to him; enjoining him to discharge the debt by a like operation, when he shall be able, and shall meet with another opportunity. I hope it may thus go thro' many hands, before it meets with a Knave that will stop its Progress. This is a trick of mine for doing a deal of good with a little money."

Inspiring people *pay it forward*, and paying it forward is about serving others.

By now, as you have worked your way through these Reflections, you will be seeing new horizons and moving even closer than before to being inspired and an inspiring person—and you will have achieved awareness of four remarkable things: 1) **The Spark:** *Why you are here,* 2) *How to build inspiring relationships,* 3) *How to create a dream,* and 4) **The Flame:** *How you will inspire others by living the* CASTLE® Principles.

Now it is time for you to pass the torch, to share what you have learned with others, to continue to inspire, coach, lead, mentor, and guide them, so that they may do the same for others, and thus change the world. This is your legacy—the legacy of an inspiring person. It is your "Ben Franklin moment."

Teaching and Coaching Changes the Future

In passing the torch to others, we become teachers, coaches, mentors, guides, and leaders and models for others. Our lives are filled with methodologies and processes aimed at supporting the growth and development of others. There is no finer teaching we can do beyond modeling what we wish others to learn. There are two traditional and widely used ways in which inspiring people do this: 1) teaching that nurtures the growth of others, and 2) mentoring and coaching them to reveal the greatness that lies within them, and all of us. But sometimes our techniques in these two areas are clumsy or ill-conceived. In some ways, teaching and coaching can even become the same thing—depending on how it is undertaken, and the circumstances involved.

Mark Twain said, "All generalizations are false, including this one," so I want to be guarded about making a generalization here. I have been coaching for many years, and I resist the notion that there are specializations in coaching—life coach, executive coach, business coach, leadership coach, career coach, spiritual coach, etc. When we teach or coach, we are addressing the whole person, not a small section of their lives. Everything is connected, as it is in all of life. If we are suffering intense back pain, it will affect the way we communicate with others, as we may become short, angry, or bilious. If we are experiencing financial pressures, we may not invest wisely in our future. If we are in a toxic relationship, it will make us miserable and we will, therefore, transfer that misery to others.

218

As I have previously emphasized, nearly everything that works well is simple, elegant, and graceful—and also wholistic and inclusive. Whenever we complicate things, we create clunkiness and inefficiency. Pseudo-sophistication in the design of processes, such as teaching or coaching, can stall the realization of a person's full potential. And complexity drains inspiration. Often, the competitive arenas of the business schools, or the consulting profession, or the school system, generate such pseudo-sophistication at the expense of simplicity, elegance, grace, and a wholistic approach. The social self wants to stand out as clever and sophisticated, so we design another theory that makes us look smart, but adds nothing to the wisdom of humanity. Simplicity rules.

Values-centered Leadership®:
The Ultimate Coaching, Teaching,
Mentoring, and Parenting Model

Whatever practical accomplishments we seek in life require the application of just three values: Mastery (doing something well), Chemistry (in a way that inspires others), and Delivery (so that we serve people and the world). The creation of an inspiring life in which we thrive and inspire others depends on these attributes.

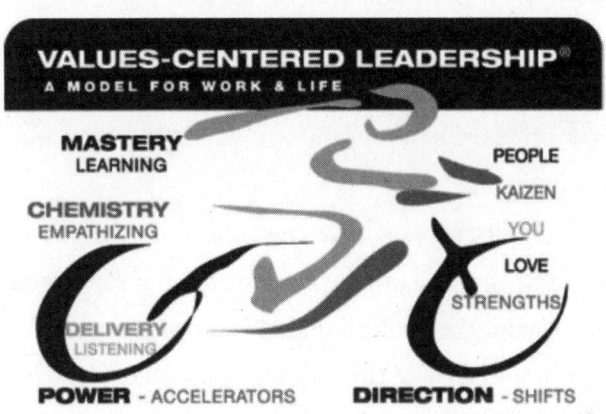

The Values-centered Leadership® Model

219

Think of a bicycle as a metaphor for your life: imagine that the processes used by you or your family, church, or organization—any group of humans—are arranged on the front and back wheels of your bicycle. Your power is derived from the back wheel and your direction from the front wheel (we will review the back wheel later in this Reflection). On the back wheel, we find the values that are the primary life skills that energize individuals, families, teams, organizations, and communities. These are called Primary Values because they help us to initiate and energize personal development and growth, change attitudes, instill self-confidence, stretch and expand our horizons, and thus positively impact ourselves and others. In other systems, too, such as teams or organizations or countries, they are a prerequisite to success. We call this model *Values-centered Leadership*®.[42]

Values-centered Leadership® is a lens through which we can view our lives and promote excellence or high performance anywhere—in our personal or professional lives, and this is achieved when we do just three things very well:

- Attain high levels of competence (**Mastery**),
- Build deep and enduring relationships (**Chemistry**), and
- Serve others (**Delivery**).

Almost any activity in which we engage can be classified under one or more of these three headings. Try thinking of something that you do in your personal or professional life that is not comfortably contained within one of these three descriptors: Mastery, Chemistry, or Delivery. These three are called the *Primary Values*.

Here are the definitions of the **Primary Values**:

- **Mastery**: *Undertaking whatever you do to the highest standards of which you are capable*
- **Chemistry**: *Relating so well with others that they actively seek to associate themselves with you*
- **Delivery**: *Identifying the needs of others, and meeting them*

Note the words used here—they have been chosen carefully. Mastery is about high standards—not Olympian, but the very best that you can accomplish with some stretching. As Ralph Waldo Emerson

---

42 To learn more about the Values-centered Leadership® Model, and the Vector 360° Leadership Survey, please visit here: https://secretan.com/higher-ground-leadership-members/vector-personal-survey/

advised us, "Our chief want in life is somebody who will make us do what we can." Chemistry describes the quality of your relationship with others—as d*efined by them*, not you. Delivery is about service, on the terms of those being served—meeting *their* needs.

Mastery

Mastery is the possession of the requisite skills, passion, and commitment to do whatever it takes to achieve high performance in a particular activity, task, or specialty. An open mind—a learner's mind—is a prerequisite. It requires a devotion to continuous personal and professional improvement, to setting standards for personal development, polishing one's skills, competencies, and practices, being an expert and respecting knowledge, wisdom, and learning. Mastery is a prerequisite for doing anything well, whether it is changing a light bulb or changing the world. Mastery embodies a commitment to excellence in how we approach things. Walt Disney used to tell his employees, "Do what you do so well that others will come to see you do it again,"—that's Mastery. Our role as inspiring individuals who coach, teach, lead, and mentor is the same: to do what we do so well that others will come to see us do it again—and to share that gift with others. Self-mastery is inspiring.

221

Mastery is a state of excellence. Ninety-eight percent of the journey to excellence is accomplished by many, but then the field narrows to those who are passionate about the last two percent. Catharine Pendrel, an Olympian cross-country mountain biker on the Canadian National Team, says, "I have that amazing race once, maybe twice a year... Afterward, I try to think back to what made everything come together. There are so many variables that this improvement, this two percent gain, could have come from any number of things. How did I travel for that event, what was my mental state, who did I travel and pre-ride with, how was my training, diet and sleep? ... Be it luck, talent, hard work, or a combination that determines success, I'll continue my search for that two percent." This is the level of passion and commitment that is shared by those in pursuit of Mastery.

Chemistry

People with excellent Chemistry develop characteristics and attitudes that lead to the building of strong relationships. They have learned, and practice, Emotional Intelligence (EQ) and Spiritual Intelligence (SQ). They place a high value on harmonious interaction with others, taking the initiative to repair, maintain, and build friendships, and they seek to fathom the depths of their relationships, going beyond the usual superficialities. They understand and relate with the *feelings* of others and connect with people at that level. They know that interest in another is the sincerest form of respect. Truthfulness and promise-keeping are keystones of Chemistry and result in the establishment of emotional bonds with others, which creates and builds on trust. Those with excellent Chemistry enjoy the company of others as much as their own, and they show genuine interest in the lives and experiences of others.

Delivery

Delivery is honoring the sacredness of others, being respectful of their needs and having a passion for meeting them. It is the graceful pursuit of service, resulting in servant-leadership and the good of the other. This focus on the needs of others can sometimes be sourced from enlightened self-interest as well as pure altruism. Delivery honors meeting the needs of people over mere self-gratification or profit-making. Delivery is founded on "win-win" negotiations and relationships that treat people—family, friends, strangers, customers, employees, suppliers—as partners, allies, and collaborators, rather than adversaries or resources to exploit, and it results in winning *with* them, not *over* them. Delivery is being concerned with doing the right thing more than doing things right.

We achieve these three Primary Values by practicing the **Accelerators**, which propel the Primary Values in this way:

- **Mastery is achieved through Learning,** defined as:
  Seeking and practicing knowledge and wisdom
- **Chemistry is achieved through Empathizing**, defined as:
  Considering the thoughts, feelings, and perspectives of others, and
- **Delivery is achieved through Listening**, defined as:
  Hearing and understanding the communications of others

223

These three are called "Accelerators" because they accelerate the Primary Value with which they are linked. For example, to achieve *greater* Mastery, we need to commit to *greater* Learning.

Though we would all like to be instantly, or easily, accomplished at Mastery, Chemistry, and Delivery, this is unrealistic. Achieving Mastery, Chemistry, or Delivery cannot be achieved by wishful thinking alone. There are concrete actions and steps that we can each take that, when purposely applied, will lead to the enhancement and growth of these three Primary Values. To achieve greater Mastery, we must engage in new Learning. Similarly, if we wish to build greater Chemistry with people, we must first Empathize with them. And meeting the needs of others—Delivery—is best achieved by Listening for those needs.

Learning

We have covered a lot of material about learning in these Reflections so far. If Mastery is chopping wood, then Learning is sharpening the ax. The dictionary defines leading as "showing the way to" and teaching as "showing how to." Therefore, leading is teaching, and teachers show learners how to learn. A teacher/leader can be more effective with a learner than with a knower—and often, our social selves trick us into becoming knowers instead of learners. Eric Hoffer has written, "In times of change, the learners will inherit the earth, while the knowers will find themselves beautifully equipped to deal with a world that no longer exists." The unevolved social self frequently sabotages learning. The knower gets stuck; the learner is open and growing.

In 1846, a young Austrian-Hungarian doctor named Ignaz Semmelweis investigated a notorious maternity ward in which nearly all the inpatients contracted a fatal case of childbed fever. During his investigations, he noticed that women who came into the ward after giving birth seldom became ill.

When a professor who cut his finger in the middle of an autopsy in that same hospital died of symptoms identical to those of these unfortunate mothers, Semmelweis reasoned that the students doing the autopsies were somehow transferring the fever to the women in the maternity ward.

Semmelweis began requiring that his students disinfect their hands before delivering babies, and the number of childbed fever cases dropped. Here is where "change" became difficult. Semmelweis was labeled insane by his colleagues for having the audacity to suggest that they should wash their hands between deliveries, and they fired him. He tried to continue his research, but was ostracized by the medical community. His own mental health eventually deteriorated, leading to his death in an insane asylum.

One final event leading to the general acceptance of germs occurred in 1860. A famed doctor was scheduled to speak at a conference at which he intended to thoroughly denounce Semmelweis's ideas. Just as he began his speech, he was interrupted by a man who proceeded to tell the audience that he had discovered the bacterium responsible for childbed fever. That man was Louis Pasteur, and the rest is history.

Lack of proper hand washing continues to be the primary reason why MRSA and other superbugs are spread in hospitals today. According to America's Center for Disease Control, one in 25 hospital patients will contract at least one infection related to hospital care alone and as many as 75,000 of them will die, adding $30 billion to the nation's health-care bill. Despite overwhelming research and evidence supporting the importance of handwashing in disease control, some physicians and clinicians still do not consider it essential to wash their hands—a knower's unwillingness to unlearn.

Change can be difficult; learning is a prerequisite, as this example shows. Sometimes, even when we are faced with indisputable evidence that should direct our actions, we will still find "the old ways" easier—this is when the knowers eclipse the learners.

For learners, greater Mastery is achieved through the natural flow of learning from masters, coaches, mentors, and leaders—in person or through their teachings. Mastery is never perfect, just as there is no perfect knowledge or wisdom. Knowledge and wisdom are always incomplete, and so continuous learning—that is, lifelong learning—is essential if continuous Mastery is to flourish in all areas of our work and personal lives. Notice that the Accelerator for Mastery is Learning, not training; training is for pets, learning is an attitude, a way of life.

In tough times—in fact, in any times—relevance, which is derived from Mastery and Learning, is essential. Survival as a species, as an individual, a family, a team, an organization, or a nation depends on relevance. When we are relevant, we inspire; when we are irrelevant, we discourage and dissuade—and eventually, we decline and die. Relevance, then, is essential to survival, at any level. We achieve this, in part, by being brilliant and masterful at whatever we do. When I walk into a coffee shop and find it empty, it is easy to see why: the place is a mess; the staff don't care, and they aren't learning; the stock is low; and it is not enticing or inspiring for me. When I walk into another coffee shop and see lines trailing out of the door, the reason is just as simple: they do what they do as well, and often much better, than anyone else—their mastery is exceptional, and it was acquired through learning. People care and brighten your day. The other day, while I was paying for my coffee in a Starbucks store, one of the baristas offered me a free sample of hot vanilla cider and a mushroom turnover. This is simple and brilliant—a demonstration of mastery and constant learning and improvement that leads to better service and an inspiring experience. Most importantly, it is relevant to *me.* Those who are masters at what they do, and are relevant themselves, are supporting the relevance of their organization, and therefore dramatically lowering their own irrelevance, which lowers the risk of being laid off in tough times.

Things change. The environment changes. People change. Tastes change. Technology and innovation changes. The game changes. Relevance means keeping up. If we aren't relevant, we become obsolete—whether we are an individual or a company. Even in tough times, if I am able, I'll find the resources to buy what you offer if it is highly relevant to who I am, what I need, and what I do.

When we focus on mastery and learning, and therefore relevance, we get better, and when we are better, we are valued, and when we are valued, we are inspired.

Empathy

Empathizing is the second Accelerator. To be a friend (Chemistry), we must "walk in the moccasins" of others, because to relate with them well, we must first understand them. This is often best achieved by imagining their feelings, emotions, and sensitivities; by thinking how we would *feel* if we were in their situation and then trying to behave as they would want us to. As Patsy Cline said, "If you can't do it with feeling, don't." So, our goal is to be in a continuous state of empathy, behaving in a way that would make each of us the kinds of people with whom we would want to be friends if our roles were reversed. This leads to great Chemistry.

Paul Levy was the CEO of Beth Israel Deaconess Medical Center in Boston when the economy crashed. His organization was savaged, and he was faced with some grim choices—revenues and costs were clearly out of balance. Fixed-thinking leaders—the knowers—in other organizations were doing what they had always done in these situations: they fired employees. But Paul Levy is a Higher Ground Leader.

Prior to making his decisions, Paul Levy spent several days visiting the people most likely to be affected by staff cutbacks. He visited the nurses' stations and noticed the staff navigating the halls with the patients in their wheelchairs. He watched them engaging, chatting, and joking with the patients, making them feel comfortable and at

ease. He watched the food staff delivering meals and being ambassa-
dors for the hospital, chatting with patients and their families. They
were, he thought, practicing medicine. As he observed these committed employees, changing beds, polishing floors, cleaning toilets,
removing trash, he realized that many were immigrants, some had
second jobs, and that their work was financially and professionally
essential to them.

As he approached the all-staff meeting at the hospital's Sherman
Auditorium to announce his plans, he saw these same people—anxious, fearful, expecting bad news—clinicians, clerical staff, ther-
apists, nurses—all vital members of an 8,000-strong team that en-
sured the smooth running of a great hospital.

He took a breath as he began. "I want to run an idea by you that I
think is important, and I'd like to get your reaction to it. I'd like to
do what we can to protect the lower-wage earners—the transporters,
the housekeepers, the food service people. A lot of these people work
really hard, and I don't want to put an additional burden on them."

Pausing, he continued, "Now, if we protect these workers, it
means the rest of us will have to make a bigger sacrifice. It means
that others will have to give up more of their salary or benefits."

Deafening sounds of grateful and sustained applause immediately filled the Sherman Auditorium. Paul Levy was flooded with
emotion. He choked up and paused. Gathering his emotions, he
explained to all these essential team members that he wanted to hear
from them with their ideas.

E-mails began pouring into Paul Levy's office—about 100 per
hour. Most of them said that they wanted to contribute to Beth Israel and would do what it took to ensure that no one lost their job.
One nurse said her team voted unanimously to forgo a three-percent
raise. An employee in the finance department, still stinging from

being laid off from his previous position at a hospital in Rhode Island, proposed a four-day week. A respiratory therapist suggested eliminating bonuses. Others volunteered to forgo vacation time and sick leave.

Paul Levy used Empathy to transform fear into inspiration. His example puts a lie to the idea that we cannot say difficult things, tell the truth, or convey bad news in ways that are inspiring—a proposition we also described in Reflection Nine: Truthfulness. *Every* communication can be an inspiring one. Empathy builds chemistry and leads to inspiration, which, in turn, raises passion and performance. The knower can't easily change, and this inflicts pain in challenging situations; the learner adapts and inspires.

Listening

229

Listening is the third Accelerator. We cannot meet the needs of others (Delivery) if we do not pause to hear what those needs are. Listening is not "not talking." To truly listen, we must shut down our "mental chatter" and genuinely, and nonjudgmentally, listen to each other. Then, and only then, can we hear each other's needs, and only then will we be able to take the appropriate actions to meet them. Of all human skills, listening is perhaps the most difficult. In one exercise that I sometimes use in my seminars, participants are divided into groups, with those in one group being required not to talk, but to only listen to those in the other group. When the listening is complete, and following some moments of silence, they may commence talking again. They always tell me how exhausting it is to spend so much time intentionally listening. This is because it is an unfamiliar activity for them—as it is for most of us. We spend much of the time when others are talking rehearsing our next great speech that we intend to deliver as soon as they are finished—sometimes even before! The fact that listening is such hard work probably explains why we do so little of it—there is a reason why we have one mouth and two ears! We are experiencing a growing social ailment—a sense that we are not being heard. It starts in our youth, with our parents and friends, and continues throughout our lives. As Will Rogers put it, "Never miss a good chance to shut up."

Not being listened to—or feeling unheard—is at the root of most arguments, failed relationships and marriages, broken friendships, politicians who disappoint, teams and leaders who fail, revolutions, strikes, resignations, and corporate collapse. Unconditional and totally attentive listening is a beautiful gift to the essential self of another. Listening is being present, more than just being silent. Arguments and conflicts are caused when people stop listening to each other, focusing instead on convincing others of their points of view, explaining them to each other in as many different ways as possible until they "win." The knower seldom listens; the learner stays curious and keeps listening. Conflicts are always resolved as soon as both parties agree only to ask questions, cease making assertions, and *listen*. We don't learn by talking; we learn by listening and enquiring. Asking questions is the first step in creating or embracing change, and listening is one of the finest forms of respect for another person. The most effective people ask better questions and therefore, if they listen, they get better answers. Stephen Hawking said, "I am just a child who has never grown up. I still keep asking these 'how' and 'why' questions. Occasionally, I find an answer."

These six little words—Mastery, Chemistry, and Delivery; and Learning, Empathizing, and Listening—are incredibly powerful because they propel all human progress, innovation, relationships, and achievements. There is nothing in the world that we cannot accomplish if we *learn* something new that leads to greater *Mastery*, *empathize* with others that leads to greater *Chemistry*, or *listen* to the needs of others to achieve greater *Delivery*. And excelling and growing in any of these combinations leads to personal inspiration and is a path towards inspiring others.

The Vector

It is possible (but not essential) to assign numerical values to questions about Mastery, Chemistry, or Delivery. For example, you might ask, "How do you feel about your mastery today?" A response might be, "It feels like around a 10 for me today." You might then ask, "What about your learning?" and the response might be, "It really feels like a 6 today." Hidden in these responses is a magic formula we call "the Vector," which the dictionary defines as "a quantity possessing both magnitude and direction." If you subtract the Primary Value (in the example above, Mastery at 10) from the Accelerator (in the example above, Learning at 6), the resulting number is −4. We call this "a negative vector of 4, as shown below

Primary Value		Accelerator		Vector
Mastery	10	Learning	6	−4

The principle behind the Vector is that the Accelerator should be greater than the Primary Value if a person wishes to develop or grow—in other words, the Accelerator must show a greater number than the Primary Value to do so. The example above suggests that there is insufficient learning to achieve greater Mastery—a 6 in learning is not sufficient to sustain a 10 in Mastery. One could go further: the current level of Mastery cannot be sustained by this lesser level of Learning because the lower power of Learning will lead to an ultimate decline in Mastery. In our different roles across all aspects of our lives—at home, or at work—as leader, coach, artisan, entrepreneur, spouse, parent, friend, or anything else—we can use this formula—the Vector—to guide us into a valuable conversation, an inspiring check-in: "What do you think you need to learn in order to achieve greater mastery?" Notice that this is a nonjudgmental, noncritical, conversational exchange designed to inform both parties and enable both to grow—based on questions, not judgments or lectures.[43]

Interpreting the Vector— The Inspiring Check-In

The Vector is a forward indicator. This makes it very different from most instruments, which are usually snapshots of history, looking back over six or 12 months, for example, and are therefore a backward indicator. On the other hand, the Vector takes account of the current situation (a Mastery level of 10 in the above example), recognizing that the current situation is simply the result of the past, and, at the same time, acknowledges that we are equally interested in the future. Furthermore, in the example above, the negative Vector of -4 predicts a future where there are insufficient levels of Learning to propel current levels of Mastery. Since the Vector is negative, it is also signaling a future decline of Mastery. This can result in a rich opportunity for deep and constructive conversation—an inspiring check-in. Since both parties are familiar with the methodology, there is no need to explain it to them; there is a natural rhythm to the conversation—a comfortable, inspiring check-in, which both parties understand to be completely constructive and forward-looking.

---

43 Check out your own levels of Mastery, Chemistry, and Delivery, and the Vector here: https://secretan.com/higher-ground-leadership-members/vector-personal-survey/

Welcome to the concept of an inspiring check-in—a non-judgmental way of conducting empathetic, inspiring conversations that are exclusively dedicated to the needs of others—at home or at work—and to providing you and them with more meaning, fulfillment, self-esteem, effectiveness, and inspiration in your work and home life.

The Shifts

The Primary Values on the back wheel provide Power and Acceleration to our lives—our families, friends, and organizations; and the values on the front wheel provide our Direction. Our motives can be enhanced by the shifts on the front wheel. Most of us are familiar, to a greater or lesser degree, with the back-wheel values; we simply need to increase our practice of them. This cannot be said of the front-wheel shifts; they are qualitatively different. Most of us are not committed practitioners of the shifts on the front wheel—in fact, we need to shift from being a knower to becoming a learner, and therefore we call the front-wheel values "shifts" because they invite us to shift from a preexisting conception to a new one. They are:

- A *shift* from me to YOU: Focusing more on the needs of others than our own
- A *shift* from things to PEOPLE: Valuing people more than material things
- A *shift* from breakthrough to KAIZEN: Celebrating the importance of doing things **better** just as much as doing them differently
- A *shift* from weaknesses to STRENGTHS: Building on our strengths just as often as searching for and criticizing weaknesses

- A *shift* from competition and fear to LOVE: Inspiring each other with love instead of fear and competition

The Definitions of the Shifts

From me to you. We are living in one of the most self-absorbed eras in human history. The personality-driven way is dangerously egocentric and counter-productive. Values-centered Leadership® is *other*-centered and seeks collaborative win-win combinations. It assumes that when we help others to grow, find fulfillment, and experience joy, we all win. It recognizes that a proposition that is good for me but bad for you is, in the end, bad for both of us—because, as we have covered several times in this book—we are one. It pursues the concept of oneness, honoring the sacredness of others and favoring a wholistic systems approach in which the members of any family, group, or team are keenly aware of their impact on all other members. The Higher Ground Leader thinks in even larger terms, because for them, *you* includes everything else—people, the environment, and the universe. To the Higher Ground Leader, the shift *from me to you* assumes that a customer is more than a walking credit card, and an employee more than a means of production, a husband or wife more than a breadwinner or homemaker, and a river more than a discharge site—because they are all you.

We are all in service, meeting the needs of family, friends, employees, customers, suppliers, communities, and our world, and if we do so brilliantly, all the time, we will be rewarded with advocates—dedicated and loyal colleagues, friends, family, and employees who no longer dread life and work, but celebrate its rewards and have fun living and doing it. In our work lives, it results in a growing crowd of customers who are fans that become our word-of-mouth

234

marketers, and a support team of suppliers who love doing business with us and partnering with us for success. More importantly, a shift from me to you offers a much-needed balance to the preoccupations flowing from our social selves, by shifting our focus from an exclusive emphasis on ego, metrics, politics, and power to the essential self and honoring the sacredness of others, serving them and our planet.

From things to people. Some of the most avaricious political and corporate leaders have established a new, and recent, low point of questing for material gain (things) at the expense of people. The genius of Western philosophy has been our unsurpassed ability to acquire, measure, analyze, and count materiality—things. But in revering analysis and acquisition, we have forgotten that all communities, families, organizations, and institutions are the sums of people, not of things. In fact, they are even more than that—they are the sums of the human spirits within them. It is the soul that inspires and becomes inspired, not things. Now, we must return to our true reason for our existence by shifting away from our unhealthy addiction to things to a renewed commitment to people. The "things" approach only obeys the social self, and bows to hierarchy, order, politics, metrics, procedures, rules, policies, manuals, formal systems, and structure. The "people" approach seeks to give preference to the essential self, to honor the heart, respect the soul, and lift the spirits of all—which automatically causes us to be more effective.

From breakthrough to kaizen. The favorite heroes of many people are breakthrough specialists—great inventors, innovators, social media influencers, creatives, artists, entrepreneurs, promoters, and marketers. They are the hares who turn their innovative breakthroughs into personal fortunes, but we need to celebrate tortoises, too—and just as passionately. As Aesop said, "Slow and steady wins the race." There are two ways to grow: through innovation and breakthrough (finding a different way) and through kaizen (finding a better way).

The capacity to do the same thing a little bit better every day may not look like a spectacular achievement in the short run, but it is in the long run. The Japanese call this *kaizen* (kai: good, and Zen: change) or "continuous improvement in personal life, home life, social life, and work life, involving everyone." But it is not simply a Japanese idea; it is an intelligent idea. It is an attitude that honors the act of micro-excellence achieved through daily personal mastery and learning.

Many people (and companies) use kaizen techniques to achieve unheard-of improvements in quality and outcomes. One of our healthcare clients used kaizen in a novel way. A very expensive liquid medication is the standard protocol for certain cancer patients receiving critical care treatment. It is contained in a plastic drip-feed bag which sits on a hangar causing gravity to propel the solution into the patient. Clinicians drain the tube before inserting it into the patient to avoid injecting air, and this wastes some of the medicine. Since it costs $100,000 per bag, waste is expensive and inefficient. A kaizen team came up with the idea of inserting a saline solution (salt water is cheap) into the drip-feed line to create the vacuum and clear the tube for the medication prior to its insertion into the patient. This way, all the medication can be delivered to the patient without any waste. Economies are achieved and, more importantly, clinical efficacy is improved—through a simple, thoughtful improvement. Big changes are often achieved this way, like the trim tab concept described earlier.

Continuous improvement (kaizen) has wider application than the workplace: it is just as important in our personal lives—in our relationships, personal growth, politics, education, health and wellness, and spiritual development. To continuously improve in every aspect of our lives is to continually grow, and this is how we remain relevant and vital. At home, an example of kaizen might be this very important question, "How might I love you more?" If we regularly ask this question of our spouse, partner, siblings, children and friends, our mutual love will inevitably grow. Kaizen is a universally applicable idea.

From weaknesses to strengths. According to Dr. Marilyn L. Kourilsky, former dean for teacher education at UCLA's Graduate School of Education, 97 percent of kindergarten children in the United States think creatively, only 3 percent form their thoughts in a conforming, structured manner. By the time they complete high school, the balance has begun to shift—46 percent think creatively, while a more rigid, structured style is preferred by 54 percent. The process of losing our individuality, passion, and creativity is completed in the workplace: by the time we are 30, a mere 3 percent enjoy the freedom of practicing holistic, original thought processes, while 97 percent of us subject all our thinking to a structure that screens for orthodoxy, social correctness, and conflict avoidance—a process for which Irving Janis coined the term "groupthink."[44] In other words, we begin our lives with a learning, open, and curious attitude, but eventually we fall under a deadening spell of creative and spiritual impotence—another example of how these qualities are already within us—we just need to remember them, burnish them, and make them a part of our lives again. In our downfall from learners

237

---

44 *Groupthink: Psychological Studies of Policy Decisions and Fiascoes,* Janis, Irving Lester; Houghton Mifflin; 2nd edition (1983)

to knowers, it is clear that we do not start out thinking like know-ers—it is something that we acquired. By criticizing, judging, and finding fault with the ideas of others, and with our own self-judge-ment, we suck the self-esteem, and inspiration, from the souls of others as well as ourselves and therefore our families and organiz-ations. Researchers claim that during an average business meeting, each idea introduced is met with nine criticisms. We pounce on our flaws, missed targets, projects that are delayed, or budget overruns, and fail to celebrate our strengths or study and perfect our successes. We tend to criticize and dwell on failings more than we build on strengths. Our news broadcasts are the same—negative news dom-inates the airwaves and the Internet, which are filled with stories of crashes, murders, violence, crime and environmental disasters, and political and corporate failures—not stories celebrating the innate goodness of humans.

By mistakenly placing our faith in the Aristotelian notion that by attacking ideas we will strengthen them, we have perfected the skills of the ego and abandoned the gifts of the soul—a triumph of the social self over the essential self. But imagine if every person and every organization devoted as much passion and time to building on their strengths, to celebrating what is working more than criticizing and judging what is not—our souls would begin healing until we became extraordinary and inspired.

Psychologist James Loehr, who has helped to train, among others, tennis great Martina Navratilova, has studied what the best tennis players do when they take a 20-second break between points dur-ing a match. Loehr discovered that mediocre players use that time to react to the previous point—scolding themselves after a missed point, for example. The best players, Loehr found, spend the time preparing for the next point, relaxing, energizing themselves, planning their strategy, and tuning their minds.

From Competition, Hostility, and Fear to Love. Much of our life is laced with metaphors of war (chocolate cake to die for; you kill me, which we reviewed in Part One). Many businesses, academic institutions, sports teams, schools and universities, and individuals dedicate enormous amounts of people-power, time, and energy to the objective of defeating opponents, crushing competitors, and creating losers. We create "war rooms," employ "road warriors," and develop "killer apps," often causing team members to feel like faux warriors on a quest to conquer competitors in the battle for advantage or market share. Of course, none of this is inspiring. It is frightening. While the social self may become animated and engaged with these metaphors, the essential self recoils. War is anathema to the soul. Life is more than an endless competition in which we are all gladiators at some level, seeking to vanquish our opponents, who, the social self conveniently forgets, are sitting at the next desk or across the breakfast table, or riding home with us on the train—they are us.

239

Life is not a battleground—it is a playground. War or the fear of losing does not inspire people. It causes us to "play not to lose" instead of "playing to win." It is more inspiring to have chocolate cake to dream for than to die for. Extraordinary accomplishments or performances are inspired and romanced from people, not beaten out of them. If we love what we do (Mastery), love the people with whom we do it (Chemistry), and love the reason for doing it (Delivery), would we still call it work? People are inspired to do what they do well by the love they feel for what they do (Mastery), the people they do it with (Chemistry), and their reasons for doing it (Delivery).

Using the Values-centered Leadership® Framework to Coach and Mentor

The front-wheel shifts, then, are modifiers for the Primary Values and Accelerators on the back wheel. For example, we might rate a "10" in Mastery as the finest heart surgeon in the world, but if we only score a "1" in the shift "from me to you," the quality of the Mastery is devalued and questionable.

Using the illustration below, here is how to build your own personal coaching plan:

1. Under the "PRIMARY VALUES" column, under "MASTERY," identify a skill, task or ability that you would like to grow over a specified time period and write this in the next column under "ASPIRATION."

2. In the next column, "STATUS TODAY 0-10", Identify the current status of this skill or ability on a scale of 0 to 10—where you stand in your journey towards realization of this aspiration—where zero is uncompleted and 10 is fully complete.

3. Under the heading "ACCELERATOR," enter the specific learning upon which you will need to embark in order to achieve the greater Mastery you have identified.

4. In the next column under "STATUS TODAY 0-10," identify the current status of your learning at this time, i.e., if all your desired learning had been completed (10), where you stand on a scale of 0 to 10, where zero is uncompleted and 10 is fully complete.

5. Finally, subtract column 6 from column 3 and enter the number in column 7 (this will result in either a positive or negative value). This is your Vector.

1	2	3 "A"	4	5 "B"	6	7 (B-A)
PRIMARY VALUES	ASPIRATION	STATUS TODAY 0-10	ACCELERATOR	ASPIRATION	STATUS TODAY 1-10	VECTOR (B-A)
MASTERY What skill do you wish to grow?	Become a better leader	6	LEARNING What will you need to learn?	Take a leadership Course	2	-4

The Vector: After you have calculated your Vector, you will be able to ask yourself questions. What do I need to do to change these numbers? A Vector is a forward indicator of the anticipated rate and direction of change, given the current levels of the Primary Value and the Accelerator and their relationship to each other—the Vector. If you subtract the Primary Value (in the example above, Mastery at 6) from the associated Accelerator (in the example above, learning at 2), the resulting number, positive or negative, (minus 4 in this example) is the Vector.

241

Complete Your Own Vector Coaching Plan[45]

Using the outline above, give some thought to your own coaching needs—become your own coach. As you articulate your own aspirations and identify the path to their achievement, you will become increasingly inspired. This will give you practice in this methodology, by helping you to gain practice working first on your own aspirations and dreams, and then, using your own experience, helping and coaching others to grow and become more inspired in their lives.

---

45 You will find a free online version of the Vector Coaching Model here: https://secretan.com/higher-ground-leadership-members/coaching-values-centered-leadership-vector/

1	2	3 "A"	4	5 "B"	6	7 (B-A)
PRIMARY VALUES	ASPIRATION	STATUS TODAY 0-10	ACCELERATOR	ASPIRATION	STATUS TODAY 1-10	VECTOR
MASTERY What skill do you wish to grow?			LEARNING What specific skills will you need to learn? What action steps will you take?			
CHEMISTRY With whom do you wish to build a stronger relationship?			EMPATHY How will you Empathize more with them?			
DELIVERY How can you be of greater service, and to whom?			LISTENING How, and to whom, will you Listen?			

All successful relationships and human actions depend on the routine practice of the back-wheel values—the combination of the Primary Values and the Accelerators. Friendships are built on them; successful parenting is strengthened by them; high performance depends on them; they define customer service and employee satisfaction; they lead to effective meetings and negotiations; marriages grow stronger through their daily use. Anywhere and anything that requires a connection with people will get stronger, and more inspiring, through the maintenance of a positive Vector.

As we pass the torch to others, helping them to grow, to become more effective, and to live fulfilling and meaningful lives, and therefore have a positive influence on the world, the Vector becomes an invaluable tool. It is nonjudgmental, other-centered, and inspiring, instead of coercive. It is calibrated against the possibilities envisioned by the other person—not the coach, mentor, or leader. It is a collaborative synthesis—of the hopes of one, and the guidance of the other—an alignment, or *attunement,* of aspirations.

The Vector conversation and coaching model is contrarian because it departs from received wisdom and breaks most of the conventional rules about personal development and coaching. Some of its unique attributes are:

1. It is a partnership conversation, not a hierarchical procedure.
2. It relies exclusively on asking questions, not on providing answers.
3. It is a dialogue between two souls, more than between two functions, titles or egos.
4. It is not demanding, intimidating, or assertive, but compassionate, supportive, and inspiring.
5. It relies more on inspiration than motivation.
6. It is not fear-based, but is founded on a loving exchange.
7. There is no possibility of failure; any aspiration that serves, leads to personal growth, and makes the world better, is a useful destination.
8. It is uniquely personal, not standardized.
9. It does not need to conform to any predetermined or universal standards, systems, or goals.
10. It has universal application—it does not need to be work-related only, but can be useful in the family or any other setting involving people; any service or growth that enhances people and the world is a valid application.
11. Goals are not the necessary condition; the only relevant criterion is personal growth—if every person grows—family, teams and organizations—then that energy can be

243

directed into higher performance and greater inspiration in life.

12. The destination for both parties is to have their respective aspirations met to the satisfaction of each—attunement.

13. Complexity represents sand in the gears; the Vector is a fundamentally simple process.

Guiding the Future

When serving others, by coaching them, mentoring, or leading, we often focus on the snapshot taken—the performance achieved in the past, or the personal accomplishments at the time. From this freeze-frame perspective, there is only a minimal view of *what the future holds*. But inspiring mentors[46] and leaders are deeply interested in passing the torch, in the *progress* of people—how they will grow and flourish in the future. The Vector is an indispensable measure of *likely* change. Assessing mastery, for example, one might enjoy a magnitude of 10 and be considered exemplary in that domain. Traditionally, we have used the current behavior as a predictor of the future, reasoning that if certain behaviors and accomplishments happened in the past, it is likely they will be repeated in the future. But this is a shaky assumption. If all we choose to see is the current value and quality of mastery, we cannot be certain about what the future holds. But if we go further, not only noting the magnitude of Mastery being 10, but *also* observing that the magnitude for Learning (the Accelerator for mastery) is 8, then we notice that this produces a negative Vector of 2, and even though the level of 10 for Mastery is outstanding, it may raise the question of whether there is insufficient power in Learning to maintain that level. In other

244

---

46 In Greek mythology, Mentor was the faithful and wise friend of Odysseus, and teacher and trusted guide to his son Telemachus.

words, while the present may appear brilliant, which is the result of everything that has gone before, the Vector can inform us that, in this case, the sustainability of this level is doubtful without a positive change in the magnitude of the Accelerator. Conversely, a magnitude of 8 for Mastery, and 10 for Learning, produces the opposite effect, yielding a positive Vector of 2, which might indicate a potential rise in the future level of Mastery—a Vector of +2. In this case, where a level of 8 for Mastery might have drawn criticism, being able to identify a level of 10 for Learning—a Vector of +2—suggests that this has already been identified and solutions are already being sought, giving us an opportunity to support future growth and inspire the individual instead of criticizing or judging the level of Mastery—working on building strengths rather than focusing on, and criticizing, weaknesses.

In this way, conversations that center on developmental questions (What would you like your Mastery to be? Do you wish to grow? Are you happy with your current level of Mastery? Do you wish to influence the magnitude of your Vector?) offer opportunities for coaching, personal development, and personal growth. They also serve to initiate a dialogue that is nurturing and inspiring and non-judgmental. This is how we inspire the world.

Postscript

• • •

The purpose of our lives and our work is more than just material or functional—it is also spiritual. An inspired life and inspiring work are the result of an inspired higher purpose, relationships, dreams, and values—and this comes from the heart. And as Ram Dass said, "When I look at the human heart, that link, that doorway, I see an institution that makes the Pentagon look like kids' toys." We don't change the world merely by going to work in the morning just to manufacture widgets or produce reports. We change the world by engaging our heart, that most amazing, complex, and powerful instrument of human potential, and we do that by *living* our Destiny, Character, and Calling—our Why-Be-Do®—by building relationships and being of service to each other, by realizing a dream, and by contributing to the healing and recovery of the planet. Each of us has chosen a different means of living, working, and connecting, using different skills, engaging with different organizations, products, and services, collaborating and living with different people, but we can all unite in a shared goal: to celebrate and honor each other and make our planet more peaceful, beautiful, and loving.

When Phil Jackson, the coach of NBA champion teams the Chicago Bulls and the Los Angeles Lakers, won his tenth NBA championship, he became arguably the greatest coach in basketball's history. Writing about that unique moment, Adrian Wojnarowski observed, "For everyone who says they would've won with Michael

Jordan and Shaquille O'Neal and [the late] Kobe Bryant, understand this: There are few coaches alive who could've commanded the respect of those players for all those years, all those championships. Maybe just one, just Jackson.

Wojnarowski describes Jackson this way: "As much as anyone, he understands that the genius of coaching isn't in the X's and O's but the humanity of it all. 'He coaches unity and chemistry and togetherness,' Bryant said. He coaches the human condition. All those coaches who say, well, give me Kobe Bryant, just understand: He [Kobe Bryant] would've eaten most of them alive."

We have danced together for twelve Reflections covering our ideas of what Kobe Bryant referred to as "unity, chemistry, and togetherness" to forge a better appreciation for becoming inspired and inspiring and living an inspired life. We have shown that to become inspired and therefore inspiring, we must find a way to light our spark. We do this by defining our Destiny, Character, and Calling—our Why-Be-Do®—having a Dream, and strengthening our relationship-building skills through the use of, among many other things, the elimination of toxic warrior language from our vocabulary. Igniting the spark means healing the past, living the present, and dreaming the future.

Then we fan the spark into a flame by practicing, and more importantly, *living* the CASTLE® Principles: Courage, Authenticity, Service, Truthfulness, Love, and Effectiveness. The flame is the brightness of how we live our lives, rather than how we talk or think about it. The flame is how we shine light upon the world and make it a better place than we found it by inspiring others.

248

It is not our words that make our flame bright so much as our deeds. As Albert Schweitzer said, "Example is not the main thing in influencing others. It is the *only* thing [italics mine]."

Finally, we pass the torch to others by coaching, mentoring, leading, and serving them, and we measure our progress as guides, and the progress of those who are new to carrying their own torch, through the Values-centered Leadership® model. And we do so by sharing what we have learned. It is how we grow—both the one with the flame, and the one with the torch. George Bernard Shaw described it this way, "If you have an apple and I have an apple and we exchange these apples, then you and I will still each have one apple. But if you have an idea and I have an idea and we exchange these ideas, then each of us will have two ideas." Thus the flame is passed to the torch.

I hope you will find that these twelve Reflections integrate comfortably into a seamless whole, enabling you to see the oneness in everything we do, honor the sacredness of others, and inspire the world. This is how we become inspired, and can therefore be inspiring for others, and thus help create a more inspiring world.

249

....

You cannot hope to build a better world without improving the individuals. To that end, each of us must work for his own improvement and, at the same time, share a general responsibility for all humanity, our particular duty being to aid those to whom we think we can be most useful.

Marie Curie

....

☑TAKE THE
PLEDGE

To be more **inspiring**
and to **inspire** one
other person today

www.inspirepledge.com